Welcome to **"Intelligent Minds: Psychology & Philosophy Trivia Book,"** a captivating journey through the realms of psychology and philosophy. This book is designed to stimulate your intellect, challenge your understanding, and spark thoughtful discussions. Whether you are a student, a professional, or simply someone with a keen interest in the workings of the human mind and the profound questions of existence, this book offers something for everyone.

Our exploration begins with the psychology of superstitions, diving into the reasons behind our irrational beliefs and how they shape our behavior. From there, we venture into the world of modern psychology, uncovering the subtle ways in which companies like Uber influence their customers and examining the complex interplay between screen time and mental health. We also delve into the fascinating quotes and life stories of influential philosophers such as Simone de Beauvoir, Socrates, Friedrich Nietzsche, John Locke, Karl Marx, and Immanuel Kant.

Each section is carefully crafted to provide insightful analysis and thought-provoking questions. We explore ethical dilemmas through the Trolley Problem, uncover the secrets of effective online selling, and investigate the powerful psychological phenomena like the placebo effect, déjà vu, and decision fatigue. Our journey also takes us through the intricate dynamics of human behavior, lying and deception, surveillance and privacy, and the philosophical explorations of justice, language, and infinity.

In addition to the detailed explorations, this book is packed with interesting facts and trivia that make the concepts more relatable and engaging. From the science behind laughter to the paradoxes of infinity, you'll find fascinating tidbits that will enhance your understanding and spark curiosity.

Whether you're flipping through for a quick read or diving deep into each topic, **"Intelligent Minds"** is designed to be both informative and entertaining. We hope this book inspires you to question, reflect, and engage in meaningful conversations about the profound and sometimes perplexing aspects of human nature and our understanding of the world.

Table of Contents

Table of Contents	3
1. The Psychology of Superstitions	5
2. How Uber Uses Psychological Tricks to Influence Its Customers	8
3. Simone de Beauvoir Through Her Quotes	10
4. Socrates: The Father of Western Philosophy	13
5. The Psychology Behind Effective Online Selling	16
6. Fact File: Why Do We Laugh? The Science of Humor	20
7. The Trolley Problem: Ethical Dilemmas	23
8. MK-Ultra	25
9. Type 1 and Type 2 Thinking	28
10. Four Types of Human Behavior	31
11. The Wild Boy of Aveyron	34
12. How Scents Influence Mood and Behavior	36
13. The Concept of the Soul	38
14. What is Truth? Epistemology	41
15. The Ethics of Genetic Engineering	43
16. Friedrich Nietzsche	45
17. Who Was John Locke?	48
18. The Philosophy of Time Travel	51
19. The Paradox of the Barber	54
20. Karl Marx Through Quotes	56
21. Understanding Phobias: Weird and Common Fears	62
22. The Psychology Behind Screen Time	65
23. Why Do We Dream? Theories and Interpretations	69
24. The Influence of Birth Order on Personality	74
25. How the Placebo Effect Works	77
26. Why Do We Have Déjà Vu?	81
27. The Concept of Infinity - A Philosophical Exploration	85
28. The Psychology of Lying and Deception	88
29. The Ethics of Surveillance and Privacy: The Edward Snowden Case	92
30. Who Was Immanuel Kant	96
31. Ancient Greek Philosophers Quiz	99
32. The Concept of Justice: A Philosophical Fact File	103
33. Priming in Marketing: Enhancing Consumer Responses	107

34. The Philosophy of Language	111
35. Who Was Confucius?	113
36. The Fascination with True Crime Stories	116
37. Sigmund Freud Through Quotes	119
38. The Stanford Prison Experiment: A Fascinating Study in Psychology	123
39. The Milgram Experiment: A Landmark Study in Psychology	127
40. The Science of Decision Fatigue	131
41. The Idea of Utopia and Dystopia	134
42. Do We Live in a Simulation? The Matrix Hypothesis	139
43. Who Was B. F. Skinner?	142
44. Psychology Quiz	145
45. The Future of Philosophy	150
46. 20 Thought-provoking philosophy questions	153
47. The Mandela Effect	156
48. The Concept of Free Will	159
59. The Hawthorne Effect	162
Thank You Note	167

1. The Psychology of Superstitions

Superstitions are beliefs or practices that stem from a desire to influence the outcome of events through seemingly irrational or non-scientific means. They often arise from the human tendency to seek patterns and meaning in a complex and unpredictable world. At their core, superstitions provide a sense of control and comfort, particularly in situations where outcomes are uncertain or beyond one's control. This psychological need for control can manifest in various forms, from simple rituals like crossing one's fingers for luck to more elaborate behaviors rooted in cultural or personal beliefs.

The origins of superstitions can be traced back to ancient civilizations, where early humans attributed natural phenomena to the actions of gods or spirits. These beliefs were reinforced through cultural transmission and storytelling, embedding superstitions deeply within societal norms. Over time, superstitions evolved, adapting to the changing cultural and social landscapes. Today, even in a scientifically advanced society, many people still hold on to superstitious practices, suggesting that these beliefs fulfill a fundamental psychological need that transcends rationality and empirical evidence.

Psychologically, superstitions can be understood through several theoretical frameworks. One key concept is the "illusion of control," where individuals overestimate their ability to influence outcomes. This is particularly evident in high-stakes or high-anxiety situations, such as sports competitions or exams, where superstitions serve as coping mechanisms to reduce stress and enhance performance. Additionally, cognitive biases, such as the confirmation bias, play a significant role in the persistence of superstitions. People tend to remember instances when a superstitious action seemed to produce a desired outcome while disregarding instances when it did not, thus reinforcing the belief.

Moreover, superstitions often thrive in environments where uncertainty and unpredictability are prevalent. For instance, in gambling, a domain characterized by chance, superstitious behaviors are rampant. This is because the randomness of outcomes fosters a psychological need to impose order and predictability. Similarly, in professional settings, rituals and superstitions can be observed, as individuals seek to navigate the complexities and pressures of their careers. Ultimately, the persistence of superstitions underscores the intricate interplay between human psychology and the quest for meaning and control in an unpredictable world.

- **Lucky Underwear:** Some athletes are so superstitious that they will wear the same "lucky" underwear for every game or match, believing it helps them win. This practice can be so ingrained that they continue wearing the same pair, even if it's worn out or tattered, just to maintain their winning streak.
- **Elevator Phobia:** In many buildings, especially in the United States, the 13th floor is often omitted. This superstition, known as triskaidekaphobia (fear of the number 13), leads to the labeling of the floors skipping directly from 12 to 14 to avoid bad luck associated with the number 13.
- **"Rabbit Rabbit":** In some English-speaking countries, people believe that saying "rabbit rabbit" as the first words on the first day of the month brings good luck for the rest of the month. This superstition is so prevalent that it has variations across different cultures and regions.
- **Breaking Mirrors:** The superstition that breaking a mirror brings seven years of bad luck dates back to ancient Rome, where it was believed that mirrors contained a piece of the user's soul. Breaking the mirror was thought to harm the soul, leading to a long period of misfortune.

"The absence of control over an important outcome creates anxiety. So, even when we know on a

rational level that there is no magic, superstitions can be maintained by their emotional benefit." - Stuart Vyse

Did You Know?

Millions of people in China believe that the color red or the number 8 will bring them wealth and happiness. Additionally, a study of consumers in Taiwan revealed that shoppers are willing to pay more money for fewer items in a package if the number of items represents a "luckier" number.

Crossed Fingers: Crossing fingers for luck originates from early Christianity, where it symbolized making the sign of the cross for protection.

Friday the 13th: Fear of Friday the 13th, known as paraskevidekatriaphobia leading some people to avoid travel or making significant decisions on this day.

Four-leaf Clovers: Finding a four-leaf clover is considered lucky with each leaf symbolizing faith, hope, love, and luck.

Knocking on Wood: The practice of knocking on wood to ward off bad luck or to prevent a jinx is believed to have originated from pagan traditions involving tree spirits.

2. How Uber Uses Psychological Tricks to Influence Its Customers

Uber leverages psychological principles to create a seamless and engaging experience for its customers, ensuring that they choose Uber time and time again. One of the key tactics is the use of dynamic pricing, commonly known as surge pricing. This strategy exploits the concept of scarcity and urgency, making customers feel that rides are in high demand and that they should book quickly before prices rise further. This sense of urgency is heightened through real-time updates and notifications, compelling users to make faster decisions, which often results in increased usage and revenue for Uber.

Another psychological tool Uber employs is the gamification of its app. Features like tracking your driver's arrival in real-time and the ability to rate your ride at the end create an interactive experience that keeps customers engaged. The rating system, in particular, taps into social validation and reciprocity principles. Riders feel compelled to leave positive feedback when they receive good service, knowing it benefits both drivers and future customers, thus fostering a community of trust and reliability.

Years ago, when people would order a taxi, they often faced anxiety with questions like "Will it turn up?" and "How long will it be?" Uber has effectively taken away that anxiety. By providing real-time updates on the driver's location and estimated arrival time, Uber gives customers a sense of control and predictability. The app's intuitive interface, with its simple design and easy navigation, reduces cognitive load, making the booking process feel effortless. Additionally, Uber's use of personalized promotions and targeted discounts, based on users' previous behaviors and preferences, creates a sense of personalized service, which enhances customer loyalty and satisfaction. By understanding and leveraging these psychological principles, Uber effectively attracts and retains its user base.

1. **Color Psychology:** Uber uses specific colors in its app design to evoke certain emotions. The predominantly black and white interface exudes sophistication and reliability, while the use of green for notifications and promotions signals action and go-ahead, subtly encouraging users to engage more with the app.
2. **Behavioral Data:** Uber collects extensive data on user behavior, including peak usage times and frequently traveled routes, to tailor their marketing efforts. This data-driven approach allows Uber to send highly personalized promotions and messages that are more likely to resonate with individual users.
3. **Psychological Pricing:** Uber employs psychological pricing strategies, such as ending fares in .99, to make prices appear lower than they actually are. This small difference can significantly impact a user's perception of cost and value, encouraging more frequent use of the service.
4. **Loss Aversion:** The app's notifications about limited-time offers or expiring discounts play on the psychological principle of loss aversion, where the fear of missing out on a deal compels users to take action quickly.
5. **Social Proof:** Uber's display of how many people are using the service in real-time, such as "X people are currently using Uber," leverages the principle of social proof. This creates a bandwagon effect, encouraging potential users to follow suit and use the service because it appears popular and trusted by others.

3. Simone de Beauvoir Through Her Quotes

Through these quotes, Simone de Beauvoir's life and character are vividly illustrated, showcasing her intellect, pioneering spirit, and enduring impact on feminist philosophy and existential thought.

"I am incapable of conceiving infinity, and yet I do not accept finity."

This quote reflects de Beauvoir's deep existential contemplation and her struggle with the concepts of existence and limitation. Born on January 9, 1908, in Paris, de Beauvoir's early life was marked by her voracious reading and intellectual curiosity. She pursued philosophy at the Sorbonne, where she met Jean-Paul Sartre, initiating a lifelong partnership that profoundly influenced her philosophical outlook and writings.

"One is not born, but rather becomes, a woman."

De Beauvoir's most famous quote encapsulates her groundbreaking analysis of gender and identity in "The Second Sex," published in 1949. This work challenged the traditional roles assigned to women and argued that gender is a social construct. De Beauvoir's commitment to feminist thought and social justice is evident in her advocacy for women's rights and her critique of the patriarchy, making her a pivotal figure in the feminist movement.

> *"To catch a husband is an art; to hold him is a job."*

This quote epitomizes de Beauvoir's critique of the societal expectations placed on women. Throughout her career, she addressed the constraints and challenges faced by women in both personal and professional spheres. Her writings and activism highlighted the need for women's independence and autonomy, emphasizing the importance of education, economic freedom, and self-determination in achieving true equality.

> *"Change your life today. Don't gamble on the future, act now, without delay."*

De Beauvoir's pragmatic approach to life and her call to action resonate in this quote. Her life was marked by an unyielding commitment to intellectual and political causes. During World War II, she was involved in the French Resistance, and post-war, she continued to advocate for various social and political issues, including women's rights and anti-colonial movements. Her courage to act and her influence as a public intellectual left an indelible mark on 20th-century thought.

Public Scandal: De Beauvoir was dismissed from her teaching position in 1943 due to accusations of corrupting minors. This scandal involved her relationships with female students, which led to legal action and widespread public scrutiny.

Open Relationship: She and Jean-Paul Sartre had a famously unconventional and open relationship. They maintained separate residences and had numerous other lovers, which they discussed openly and included in their philosophical discussions.

Crossing Paths with Albert Camus: De Beauvoir and Sartre had a complex relationship with fellow existentialist philosopher Albert Camus. Initially friends and collaborators, their relationship soured over political and ideological differences, particularly after Camus criticized communism.

Literary Prodigy: De Beauvoir published her first novel, "She Came to Stay," in 1943. The novel is a fictionalized account of her and Sartre's relationship with one of her students, showcasing her ability to blend her philosophical ideas with narrative storytelling.

World Traveler: De Beauvoir was an avid traveler, documenting her experiences in works such as "America Day by Day" and "The Mandarins." Her travels took her around the globe, including extended stays in the United States, China, and Latin America, influencing her worldview and writings

Did You Know?

Simone de Beauvoir's impact extended beyond her philosophical and literary achievements into the realm of advocacy and social change. She was a vocal supporter of decolonization movements in Africa and Asia, aligning herself with anti-colonial struggles for independence. De Beauvoir's travels, particularly to countries like Algeria and China, shaped her understanding of global power dynamics and oppression. Her observations and reflections during these journeys influenced her later writings, where she critiqued imperialism and advocated for the rights of colonized peoples. This aspect of her activism underscores her commitment to justice and equality on a global scale.

4. Socrates: The Father of Western Philosophy

Socrates (470/469 – 399 BCE) was an ancient Greek philosopher who is widely regarded as one of the founding figures of Western philosophy. He was born in Athens and lived during a time of significant cultural and intellectual development in Greece. Despite not leaving behind any written works, Socrates' ideas and methods have had a profound and lasting impact on philosophy and intellectual history.

Socrates is best known for his distinctive method of inquiry, now called the Socratic method, which involves asking a series of probing questions to stimulate critical thinking and illuminate ideas. This method aims to expose contradictions in the interlocutor's thoughts and lead them to a clearer understanding of the subject under discussion. Socrates believed that through dialogue and questioning, individuals could attain true knowledge and wisdom.

One of the most important sources of information about Socrates is the work of his student Plato. In Plato's dialogues, Socrates is often depicted engaging in philosophical discussions with various Athenians, exploring topics such as justice, virtue, and the nature of knowledge. Another student, Xenophon, also wrote about Socrates, providing additional insights into his life and philosophy.

Socrates' commitment to questioning established norms and his belief in the examined life ultimately led to his trial and execution. In 399 BCE, he was accused of corrupting the youth of Athens and impiety (disrespecting the gods of the city). Despite his defense, Socrates was found guilty and sentenced to death by drinking a cup of poison hemlock. His death is often seen as a powerful statement about the pursuit of truth and intellectual integrity, marking him as a martyr for philosophy.

Socrates' legacy endures through the works of Plato and other philosophers who were influenced by his ideas. His emphasis on critical thinking, ethical living, and the pursuit of knowledge continues to inspire and shape philosophical thought to this day.

- **No Written Works:** Despite his profound influence on philosophy, Socrates himself never wrote any texts. All that is known about his teachings comes from the writings of his students, primarily Plato and Xenophon.
- **Oracle's Pronouncement:** The Oracle of Delphi once declared that Socrates was the wisest man in Athens. Socrates interpreted this to mean that true wisdom comes from recognizing one's own ignorance, leading to his famous assertion, "I know that I know nothing."
- **Physical Appearance:** Unlike the typical portrayal of philosophers as dignified figures, Socrates was known for his distinctively unattractive appearance. He had a flat nose, bulging eyes, and was often described as looking more like a satyr than a revered thinker.
- **Military Service:** Socrates served as a hoplite (a heavily armed foot soldier) in the Athenian army. He fought in several significant battles during the Peloponnesian War, including the Battle of Potidaea, the Battle of Delium, and the Battle of Amphipolis, demonstrating considerable bravery.
- **Barefoot Philosopher:** Socrates was known for his ascetic lifestyle, often walking barefoot and wearing the same simple cloak year-round, regardless of the weather. His indifference to material wealth and physical comfort was a testament to his philosophical beliefs.
- **Strange Behavior:** Socrates sometimes exhibited peculiar behavior. For example, he could stand still for hours, deep in thought, oblivious to his surroundings. This intense focus on contemplation was a hallmark of his dedication to philosophy.

- **Influence on Stoicism:** Socrates' emphasis on ethics and the pursuit of virtue greatly influenced later philosophical traditions, particularly Stoicism. The Stoic philosophers admired his commitment to living a virtuous life in accordance with reason.
- **Marital Challenges:** Socrates' wife, Xanthippe, is often portrayed as a shrewish and difficult woman. Their relationship was famously tumultuous, and stories of her temper have been passed down through the ages. Despite this, Socrates viewed her challenging nature as a way to build his patience and character.

Death with Dignity

When Socrates was sentenced to death, he had the opportunity to escape with the help of his friends. They had arranged for his escape from prison, providing a chance for him to flee and avoid his unjust execution. However, Socrates chose to accept his fate, adhering to his principles and beliefs about justice and the rule of law. He argued that escaping would undermine the laws of Athens and contradict the philosophical principles he had lived by. His acceptance of the death sentence, even when faced with an easy escape, demonstrated his unwavering commitment to his beliefs and became a powerful statement about the pursuit of truth and intellectual integrity. Socrates' decision to drink the hemlock, rather than flee, solidified his legacy as a martyr for philosophy and a symbol of moral integrity.

5. The Psychology Behind Effective Online Selling

The world of online selling is drowning in data. From analytics dashboards to visualization tools to A/B testing suites to automated marketing solutions, just keeping your head above the big-data waters can be overwhelming. Sadly, even with this flood of computer-generated insights, 95.8% of the world's internet users still do "nothing" when they visit a site.

So, what's missing? Psychology. As Neil Patel puts it in "The Complete Guide to Understand Customer Psychology": "Online marketers are obsessed with traffic acquisition numbers and conversion rates. It's easy to forget that your consumers are real people on the other side of the computer screen." The key to reaching these "real people" is triggering what persuasion expert Robert Cialdini calls "judgmental heuristics" in his book "Influence: Science and Practice." Heuristics are "mental shortcuts" that allow you to take advantage of humanity's love of "simplified thinking." Cialdini identified six "weapons of influence," which form the basis for effective psychological marketing strategies. Below are these principles, enhanced with practical tips and real online examples.

1. Reciprocity

Reciprocity is a powerful and deeply ingrained psychological trigger. The principle is simple: when you receive, you're more likely to give. This isn't just fanciful karma. As Cialdini explains, "One of the most widespread and basic norms of human culture is embodied in the rule for reciprocation. The rule requires that one person try to repay, in kind, what another person has provided."

To trigger reciprocity online, offering "lead magnets" or "carrot content offers" such as free email series, online courses, webinars, whitepapers, checklists, or special reports is effective. For example, QuickSprout's "Free Course" serves as their primary call-to-action (CTA). Similarly, SaaS companies use the "freemium" model. Dropbox, for instance, grew from 50 million users in 2010 to over 300 million by offering 2GB of free space, with paid plans starting at $9.99/month. Although only 4% of users were paid subscribers in 2011, this translated into upwards of $1.18 billion in annual revenue.

2. Scarcity

Scarcity drives consumer behavior by creating a sense of urgency and the fear of missing out (FOMO). The harder it is to get something, the more we want it. This principle is evident in the surge in gun sales following calls for more restrictive gun laws in the US.

Online, scarcity can be created through tactics like limited availability and time-sensitive offers. Amazon often displays messages like "Only 9 left in stock" and "Order within 2 hrs 50 mins and choose One-Day Shipping at checkout." Similarly, free trials leverage scarcity by allowing customers to experience a product or service, making them more likely to pay to avoid losing access.

3. Consistency and Commitment

Consistency and commitment operate on two levels. First, people prefer to act in ways that are consistent with their past behavior. Second, small commitments lead to larger ones. For instance, Conversion Voodoo increased application conversion rates by over 11% simply by adding a commitment checkbox.

Two-step opt-in forms, like those used by LeadPages, break the sign-up process into smaller steps, leading to a 60% increase in opt-ins. Retargeting ads, which follow users based on their website visits, can boost response rates by up to 400% compared to cold ads.

4. Authority

Authority utilizes the power of specific individuals or symbols to influence behavior. People respond to the appearance of authority, such as endorsements from medical professionals or celebrities. However, if hiring celebrities isn't feasible, logos of well-known companies or media appearances can serve the same purpose.

For example, Coding Zeal features clients' logos on their site, and Ramit Sethi uses logos of media outlets where he has been featured. This tactic conveys authority and builds trust with potential customers.

5. Liking

People prefer to say yes to individuals they know and like. Building rapport through shared interests, similarities, and compliments is crucial. For example, Airbnb revamped its referral program based on the principle of liking, resulting in a 300% increase in user signups and bookings per day.

Creating relatable "About Pages" can also build a connection with visitors. ProBlogger Darren Rowse's story resonates with his audience, making his site more engaging and trustworthy.

6. Clustering

Clustering helps people retain information by grouping similar items together. This principle is useful for making content more scannable and memorable through headings, bulleted lists, and background changes.

Tiered pricing structures also benefit from clustering. Presenting high, medium, and low options makes comparisons easier and choices clearer, often driving customers to select the middle option.

7. Social Proof

Social proof leverages the influence of crowds by using testimonials, endorsements, and ratings from real people. Harvard Business School found that a one-star increase in Yelp ratings leads to a 5-9% increase in revenue for independent restaurants.

Including testimonials on checkout pages, like Ancestry.com does, can significantly enhance conversions. Positive social media mentions and in-depth case studies also provide powerful social proof.

Did You Know?

TripAdvisor has fundamentally transformed how travelers make decisions, becoming a cornerstone of the tourism industry through its extensive use of social proof. With over 884 million reviews and opinions covering 8.9 million accommodations, restaurants, and attractions worldwide, TripAdvisor has become a go-to platform for travelers seeking reliable insights from fellow globetrotters. Research indicates that 53% of travelers won't book a hotel without reading reviews first, underscoring the platform's influence on consumer behavior. Moreover, TripAdvisor's ranking algorithms, which consider both quality and quantity of reviews, ensure that establishments with positive social proof are prominently featured, further enhancing their appeal to potential customers. This emphasis on social proof not only guides travelers in making informed choices but also empowers businesses to leverage positive reviews as a competitive advantage, illustrating the profound impact of peer feedback on the travel industry's digital landscape.

6. Fact File: Why Do We Laugh? The Science of Humor

- **Brain Activation**: Activates multiple brain regions, including the frontal lobe.
- **Neurotransmitters**: Releases endorphins and dopamine, associated with happiness and pleasure.
- **Bonding Mechanism**: Strengthens social bonds and fosters a sense of community.
- **Social Signals**: Signals trust, cooperation, and shared understanding within a group.
- **Stress Reduction**: Reduces levels of cortisol and adrenaline, leading to relaxation and reduced anxiety.
- **Mood Enhancement**: Regular laughter boosts mood and helps combat symptoms of depression.
- **Immune Function**: Boosts the immune system by increasing antibody production and activating immune cells.
- **Pain Relief**: The release of endorphins acts as a natural painkiller, providing temporary relief from discomfort.
- **Incongruity Theory**: Humor arises from recognizing incongruity or the unexpected, triggering laughter.
- **Cognitive Shift**: Requires viewing a situation from a different perspective, appreciating absurdity or surprise.
- **Survival Mechanism**: Evolved to signal safety and promote group cohesion, crucial for cooperation and social living.
- **Mate Selection**: Ability to make others laugh indicates intelligence and social adeptness, seen as desirable traits.
- **Universality**: Basic act of laughing is universal, but what people find funny varies across cultures.
- **Cultural Norms**: Cultural context shapes humor, with certain jokes resonating more within specific settings.

- **Early Development**: Babies start to laugh at around 3-4 months old, indicating early developmental milestone.
- **Learning through Play**: Children use laughter and humor in play to learn about social roles, rules, and boundaries.
- **Therapeutic Practice**: Laughter yoga combines voluntary laughter with yoga breathing exercises for health benefits.
- **Global Movement**: Laughter yoga promotes health and wellness through structured sessions, originating in India.
- **Psychological Interventions**: Humor is used in therapy, including CBT and positive psychology, to cope with emotions.
- **Emotional Release**: Provides an emotional release, helping individuals deal with grief, trauma, and stress.

Study Spotlight: Laughter and Pain Tolerance

Study Overview Researchers from the University of Oxford conducted a study to investigate the relationship between laughter and pain tolerance. The study aimed to understand how laughter influences our physical experience of pain and the underlying mechanisms at play.

Methodology The study involved 92 participants who were divided into two groups. One group watched 15 minutes of comedy videos, while the other group watched 15 minutes of neutral content, such as documentaries. Before and after the viewing sessions, participants underwent a series of pain threshold tests, including placing their arms in cold water and having a blood pressure cuff inflated to painful levels.

Findings The results showed that participants who watched the comedy videos experienced a significant increase in pain tolerance compared to those who watched the neutral content. The comedy group reported feeling less pain and were able to endure the pain tests for longer periods.

Explanation The researchers attributed the increased pain tolerance to the release of endorphins triggered by laughter. Endorphins are natural painkillers produced by the brain that can induce a feeling of euphoria and relaxation. The social bonding aspect of shared laughter may also play a role in enhancing pain tolerance, as it promotes a sense of well-being and connectedness.

Did You Know?

- During the 7 minutes of neural activity before dying, you will see your memories in a dreamlike pattern.
- Having siblings is proven to help with getting along well with peers.
- The way an individual treats the employees at an establishment tells immensely about their character.
- If you sob out of happiness, the first tear will come from the right eye, but if you cry out of sorrow, it will come from the left.
- Food prepared by someone else tastes much better than your preparation, even when you use the same recipe.
- Hearing a single negative thing could damage at least five positive memories.
- Studies have shown that consuming food without preservatives will increase I.Q by up to 14%.
- You seem to think more about a specific individual than about catastrophic events.
- An individual still has 7 minutes of neural activity before he passes away.
- Researchers have observed that thinking that something bad is going to happen is less stressful to understand than not understanding how it will eventually wind up.
- Another interestingly fun fact about psychology is that it keeps us fascinated as humans are always curious about knowing their minds better!

7. The Trolley Problem: Ethical Dilemmas

The Trolley Problem is a classic ethical dilemma in moral philosophy that explores the conflict between utilitarian and deontological ethical theories. Originating from the work of philosopher Philippa Foot in the 1960s, it presents a scenario where a runaway trolley is headed towards five people tied to a track. You, as an observer, have the power to pull a lever that will divert the trolley onto another track, where only one person is tied. The dilemma forces you to choose between actively causing one person's death to save five others or passively allowing the five to die.

In the initial scenario, the decision seems to revolve around a straightforward utilitarian calculation: sacrificing one life to save five maximizes overall happiness and minimizes suffering. This perspective aligns with the principle of utilitarianism, which suggests that the morally right action is the one that produces the greatest good for the greatest number. By pulling the lever, you actively minimize the total harm, making the choice appear ethically justifiable from a utilitarian standpoint.

However, the Trolley Problem becomes more complex when considering deontological ethics, which focuses on the morality of actions themselves rather than their consequences. From a deontological perspective, intentionally causing harm to an innocent person is inherently wrong, regardless of the outcome. Pulling the lever, in this view, would make you morally responsible for the death of the one person, violating the ethical duty not to harm others. This perspective challenges the straightforward utilitarian solution, emphasizing the moral significance of individual rights and the integrity of moral principles.

The problem extends into various nuanced scenarios to further test moral intuitions. For instance, consider the "Fat Man" variation, where instead of pulling a lever, you must push a large man off a bridge to stop the trolley and save the five people. This version intensifies the moral conflict, as it requires a more direct and personal action to achieve the same utilitarian outcome. Most people find this act more morally troubling, suggesting that the method of intervention affects our ethical judgments. This variation highlights the importance of the means by which an outcome is achieved in ethical decision-making.

Moreover, the Trolley Problem has practical implications in contemporary ethical discussions, such as autonomous vehicle programming, medical ethics, and wartime decisions. For example, how should self-driving cars be programmed to handle situations where harm is unavoidable? Should they follow utilitarian principles and minimize total harm, or should they adhere to deontological rules that prioritize not causing direct harm? These real-world applications underscore the relevance and urgency of the ethical questions posed by the Trolley Problem, demonstrating its significance beyond theoretical debates.

In conclusion, the Trolley Problem serves as a powerful tool for examining the complexities of moral decision-making. It challenges individuals to consider the implications of their ethical beliefs and the potential conflicts between different moral frameworks. By exploring the tension between utilitarian and deontological ethics, the Trolley Problem illuminates the intricacies of ethical dilemmas and encourages deeper reflection on what it means to act morally. As such, it remains a vital topic in both philosophical inquiry and practical ethical discussions.

8. MK-Ultra

The story of the CIA's use of LSD, known as MK-Ultra, is a complex and controversial chapter in the history of intelligence agencies and psychological experimentation. In the 1950s and 1960s, during the Cold War era, the CIA became interested in the potential of mind control techniques for interrogation and espionage purposes.

Under MK-Ultra, the CIA conducted a wide range of experiments involving psychedelic drugs like LSD, as well as other methods such as hypnosis and sensory deprivation. The goal was to explore the effects of these substances on human behavior, including their potential for interrogation, mind control, and covert operations.

One infamous aspect of MK-Ultra involved administering LSD to unsuspecting individuals, including volunteers, military personnel, prisoners, and even some CIA agents themselves. These experiments often took place without the subjects' consent or knowledge, leading to profound and sometimes dangerous psychological effects.

One of the most well-known cases of LSD experimentation under MK-Ultra was the case of Frank Olson, a scientist working for the CIA. In 1953, Olson was unknowingly dosed with LSD during a CIA retreat, which resulted in a severe psychotic episode. A few days later, Olson plunged to his death from a hotel window in New York City, under circumstances that remain controversial and subject to speculation.

As details of MK-Ultra began to emerge through investigations and congressional hearings in the 1970s, the program came under intense scrutiny and criticism. It was revealed that the CIA had engaged in unethical and often illegal activities, violating human rights and medical ethics standards. In 1973, CIA Director Richard Helms ordered the destruction of most MK-Ultra documents, further obscuring the full extent of the program's activities.

- In the early 1950s, the CIA, under Sidney Gottlieb's leadership, acquired the **world's entire supply of LSD** with an investment of $240,000, a substantial sum at the time.
- In a profound twist of fate, the CIA's MK-Ultra program, while aiming to harness LSD as a tool for mind control and interrogation, inadvertently ignited a cultural revolution.
- Key figures like Ken Kesey, Robert Hunter, and Allen Ginsberg were among those who participated in CIA-sponsored LSD experiments without their knowledge of the agency's involvement. Kesey, an influential author, and Hunter, a pivotal lyricist for the **Grateful Dead**, along with Ginsberg, a leading poet of the time, went on to play monumental roles in promoting LSD culture. Their experiences under these experiments, perceived as profound and pleasurable, were shared widely, thus fueling a counter-cultural movement that stood in stark opposition to the very values the CIA sought to protect.
- The irony could not be more striking—the CIA, in attempting to control human consciousness through LSD, ended up providing the catalyst for a societal shift that celebrated free thought and rebellion against authoritative structures. This generational movement was inherently aligned against the principles and methods of the CIA, championing personal freedom and questioning of governmental authority.
- **Whitey Bulge**r, a notorious crime boss, serves as a stark example of the darker side of these experiments. Told he was participating in research to cure schizophrenia, Bulger was administered LSD daily for over a year. This manipulation revealed the extreme lengths to which MK-Ultra went to test the effects of prolonged LSD exposure, aiming to see if it could break down an individual's psychological stability. Bulger's later realization of his role as a mere 'guinea pig' in a sinister governmental plot highlights the ethical breaches committed under the guise of scientific research.

Another notable CIA project that shares similarities with MK-Ultra, Operation Artichoke, and Project Bluebird is **Project Stargate**.

Project Stargate, also known as **Scanate**, was a secret program that focused on the potential military and intelligence applications of psychic phenomena such as remote viewing. It was active from the 1970s through the 1990s and aimed to investigate whether individuals could use extrasensory perception (ESP) or psychic abilities to gather intelligence about remote targets.

Under Project Stargate, trained individuals known as remote viewers attempted to gather information about designated targets, including foreign military installations, hostages, and other classified locations, using their purported psychic abilities. The CIA and other agencies conducted research and experiments to assess the validity and reliability of these techniques, often in collaboration with scientists and psychologists.

Like MK-Ultra and its predecessors, Project Stargate operated under secrecy and attracted controversy due to its unconventional methods and claims regarding psychic abilities. While some proponents argued for the potential utility of remote viewing in intelligence operations, skeptics questioned its scientific basis and ethical implications, particularly regarding the treatment of individuals involved in the program.

In 1995, following public scrutiny and internal evaluations, the CIA declassified documents related to Project Stargate, shedding light on its activities and the motivations behind exploring unconventional intelligence-gathering methods. The project remains a subject of interest and debate among researchers, historians, and those interested in the intersection of intelligence operations and paranormal phenomena.

9. Type 1 and Type 2 Thinking

Type 1 Thinking: Intuitive and Fast

Type 1 thinking operates automatically and quickly, with little or no effort and no sense of voluntary control. It involves making split-second decisions based on instinct and gut reactions.

- **Examples**: Recognizing faces, understanding simple sentences, and detecting hostility in someone's voice are all tasks managed by Type 1 thinking.
- **Advantages**: It helps us respond quickly in situations where speed is more valuable than accuracy, such as avoiding immediate dangers.
- **Limitations**: While efficient, Type 1 thinking can lead to biases and errors because it relies heavily on associative memory and familiar patterns, often ignoring logical analysis.

Type 2 Thinking: Analytical and Slow

Type 2 thinking allocates attention to effortful mental activities that demand it, including complex computations. The operations are often slower, associated with the subjective experience of agency, choice, and concentration.

- **Examples**: Focusing on a challenging math problem, evaluating the pros and cons of a major decision, and engaging in strategic planning are all driven by Type 2 thinking.
- **Advantages**: This type of thinking allows for deeper and more rational analysis, leading to more accurate judgments and decisions in complex situations.

- **Limitations**: Type 2 thinking requires more energy and time, making it less practical for everyday decisions and often overridden by the faster and more automatic Type 1 thinking in routine situations.

Interaction Between Type 1 and Type 2 Thinking

Balancing Act

In daily life, both types of thinking interact seamlessly. Type 1 offers a first reaction to stimuli, which Type 2 can either endorse by taking no action or override by engaging in deeper analysis and questioning.

Error Checking

Type 2 thinking often serves as a check on Type 1 processes, stepping in when decisions require more accuracy, such as revising initial judgments or solving problems that arise from intuitive responses.

> *"When faced with a difficult question, we often answer an easier one instead, usually without noticing the substitution."*

Neurological Bases: Studies using functional MRI scans have shown that different brain regions are activated during Type 1 and Type 2 thinking. For instance, the amygdala plays a crucial role in fast, emotion-driven responses typical of Type 1 thinking, while the frontal lobes are more active during the deliberate and analytical tasks of Type 2 thinking.

Decision Fatigue: Engaging in prolonged periods of Type 2 thinking can lead to decision fatigue, a state where the brain tires and begins to seek shortcuts. This often results in either decision avoidance or a reversion to Type 1 thinking, which can be less taxing but more prone to errors.

> *"We easily think associativity, we think metaphorically, we think casually, but stats requires thinking about many things at once, which is something that System 1 (fast thinking) is not designed to do."*

Impact of Stress: Stress can significantly impact the balance between Type 1 and Type 2 thinking. Under high stress, the brain is more likely to favor Type 1 thinking for quick decision-making, which can be beneficial in immediate danger but detrimental in complex, non-emergency situations.

> *"Intelligence is not only the ability to reason; it's also the ability to find relevant material in memory and to deploy attention when needed.*

Age and Cognitive Development: The efficiency and preference for Type 1 versus Type 2 thinking can change with age. Children and older adults tend to rely more on Type 1 thinking, while adults in their prime working years may be more adept at engaging in Type 2 thinking.

10. Four Types of Human Behavior

In any professional setting, understanding and recognizing the diverse behavioral styles of coworkers and clients can significantly enhance communication and foster a productive workplace environment. Broadly categorized into four types—Analytical, Amiable, Driver, and Expressive—each behavioral style has unique characteristics and communication needs. Knowing how to interact with each type can lead to more effective collaborations and business outcomes. Here's a concise introduction to these four behavioral types, providing insights on how to tailor communication to match each style effectively.

- **Analytical Characteristics:** Detail-oriented, cautious, and methodical, analytical types value precision and structured information. Communication Tips: Use clear, well-organized arguments, avoid emotional language, provide data and facts to support your points.
- **Amiable Characteristics:** Warm, friendly, and supportive, amiable individuals prioritize relationships and consensus. Communication Tips: Use a personal approach, express interest in them and their ideas, ensure a non-threatening environment.
- **Driver Characteristics:** Goal-oriented, decisive, and efficient, drivers are focused on achieving results quickly. Communication Tips: Be brief, direct, and to the point, focus on objectives and efficiency, respect their time.
- **Expressive Characteristics:** Energetic, imaginative, and spontaneous, expressive types are great at motivating others and fostering enthusiasm. Communication Tips: Be engaging

and expressive, allow them to share ideas and feelings, appreciate their creativity and insights.

But Wait, There's a Twist!.....

Let's take a moment to mix things up a bit. While it's useful to understand the four main behavior types, it's important to remember that people aren't limited to just one category. We're more like a complex blend of characteristics, often displaying traits from different styles depending on the situation. So, as you navigate through these types, think of them as guidelines, not strict labels. Everyone brings their own unique blend to the table, making human behavior a fascinatingly nuanced puzzle. Keep this in mind, and you'll find that understanding others is not just insightful, but also more accurate.

"Communication happens on the listener's terms" — Thomas Erikson, Surrounded by Idiots

- Analytical types tend to excel in roles that require meticulous planning and detailed analysis. Their ability to delve deep into data makes them exceptional candidates for positions in finance, research, and strategic planning, where precision is paramount.
- Amiable individuals are often successful in roles that require a high degree of teamwork and collaboration. Their empathetic nature and ability to maintain interpersonal relationships make them effective team leaders and valuable in roles within human resources and customer service.
- Driver types are naturally suited for executive and managerial roles where quick decision-making and goal orientation are crucial. Their ability to see the big picture and push forward on initiatives makes them powerful leaders, particularly in startup and sales environments

- Expressive individuals thrive in environments that require innovation and communication. They are often found excelling in marketing, public relations, and other creative roles where their energy and ability to engage others can be fully utilized.
- Individuals who exhibit traits from multiple personality types often excel in roles that require versatility, such as project management or client-facing positions. Their ability to adapt and leverage different strengths allows them to navigate complex environments effectively.

The Behavioral Symphony: Imagine a workplace where each behavioral type is like a different instrument in a symphony orchestra. The Analyticals are the meticulous violinists, meticulously tuning their facts and figures. Amiables are the harmonious cellists, weaving relationships into every interaction like strands of melody. Drivers are the bold conductors, wielding their batons decisively to drive the team towards success. And Expressives? They're the charismatic trumpeters, injecting bursts of creativity and energy into the workplace ensemble. Together, they create a harmonious blend of precision, empathy, efficiency, and enthusiasm, each note contributing to the grand symphony of organizational achievement. Understanding this dynamic orchestra not only enriches workplace interactions but also ensures that every performance—every project—is a masterpiece of collaboration and synergy.

11. The Wild Boy of Aveyron

In 1800, a mysterious boy estimated to be about 11 or 12 years old was discovered emerging alone from the forests of Aveyron, France. Named Victor by his caretakers, he appeared to have spent most of his early life in the wild, devoid of any human contact, and lacked the ability to speak or understand language. Despite numerous efforts by caregivers and scientists, Victor never acquired the ability to speak fluently, sparking debates about the critical period for language development. While he gradually learned some aspects of social behavior such as wearing clothes and basic hygiene, Victor remained largely disconnected from deep human interaction.

Victor's case became a foundational study in the debate over nature versus nurture, exploring the impact of genetics versus environment on human behavior and development. Early investigations into his condition also contributed to the field of autism research. Though the term "autism" was not used at the time, later interpretations by experts like Uta Frith suggested that Victor might have displayed traits consistent with autism spectrum disorders. The observations and studies conducted on Victor provided significant insights into human development and the potential for learning and adaptation despite severe early deprivation.

Lean Marc Gaspard Itard, the physician who took Victor under his care, developed innovative educational methods through his work with Victor. These methods laid the groundwork for future strategies in educating individuals with developmental challenges. Victor's story gained further recognition with the 1970 French film adaptation directed by François Truffaut, who also played the role of Dr. Jean Itard. The film focused on the challenges and ethical questions involved in trying to "civilize" Victor and was acclaimed for its thoughtful exploration of human nature and socialization.

- **Documentary Evidence**: Victor's discovery and subsequent life were well-documented by his caregivers, providing a rare and detailed case study of a feral child in historical records.
- **Influence on Education**: Itard's work with Victor influenced the development of special education, particularly methods used for teaching children with hearing impairments and developmental disorders.
- **Public Fascination**: Victor's story captivated the public and scientific community of his time, leading to numerous publications and discussions about human nature, the origins of language, and the effects of isolation on development.

""In the story of Victor, we glimpse both the depths of human resilience and the profound mysteries of our capacity for language and socialization. His life challenges us to reconsider the boundaries of nature and nurture, reminding us that even in the face of profound isolation, there remains an indomitable spirit yearning for connection."

12. How Scents Influence Mood and Behavior

Scents have a profound impact on our mood and behavior, often influencing our emotions and actions in ways we might not even realize. The olfactory system, which processes smells, is directly linked to the limbic system in the brain, a region involved in emotion and memory. This connection explains why certain scents can evoke vivid memories or strong emotional responses. For instance, the smell of freshly baked cookies might transport someone back to their childhood, evoking feelings of comfort and nostalgia.

Research has shown that specific scents can have predictable effects on mood and behavior. For example, the scent of lavender is well-known for its calming properties. Studies have demonstrated that lavender can reduce anxiety, improve mood, and even enhance sleep quality. In contrast, invigorating scents like peppermint can increase alertness and improve cognitive performance. This has practical applications in environments where focus and concentration are required, such as workplaces or educational settings.

In addition to mood, scents can also influence behavior. Retailers often use scent marketing to create a specific atmosphere or to encourage certain behaviors among customers. A pleasant scent in a store can enhance the shopping experience, making customers more likely to linger and make purchases. For example, studies have found that the scent of vanilla can create a sense of relaxation and comfort, leading to longer shopping times and increased sales. Similarly, the scent of citrus has been shown to promote a clean and energetic atmosphere, which can positively affect customers' perceptions of a store.

The impact of scents on mood and behavior is also leveraged in therapeutic settings. Aromatherapy, which uses essential oils to promote physical and emotional well-being, is a popular complementary therapy. Oils like eucalyptus are used to relieve respiratory issues, while scents like chamomile are used to reduce stress and promote relaxation. The effectiveness of aromatherapy highlights the powerful connection between our sense of smell and our overall health and well-being.

1. **Hospital Recovery**: Studies have shown that patients in hospitals recover more quickly when exposed to pleasant scents. For example, a study found that patients exposed to the scent of lavender experienced less pain and required fewer pain medications after surgery.
2. **Improved Sports Performance**: Research indicates that certain scents can enhance athletic performance. The scent of peppermint has been found to increase physical performance, reduce perceived effort, and improve overall motivation during exercise.
3. **Memory Enhancement**: The scent of rosemary has been linked to improved memory and cognitive function. One study revealed that students who were exposed to the scent of rosemary essential oil while studying performed better on memory tests compared to those who were not.
4. **Stress Reduction in High-Traffic Areas**: In Japan, some companies have introduced scent diffusers in high-stress work environments, such as call centers and busy offices. Scents like lemon and lavender are used to reduce stress levels and improve employee well-being and productivity.

13. The Concept of the Soul

The concept of the soul has fascinated humanity for millennia, encompassing a wide range of interpretations across different cultures, religions, and philosophies. At its core, the soul is often considered the essence of a person, representing their true self beyond the physical body. While the specifics of what the soul entails and its implications vary greatly, the underlying idea is that it is an immortal, spiritual component distinct from the material world.

In ancient Greek philosophy, the soul (psyche) was a fundamental element of human existence. Plato viewed the soul as immortal, pre-existing before birth and continuing after death. He proposed that the soul is divided into three parts: the rational, the spirited, and the appetitive. The rational soul seeks truth and wisdom, the spirited soul strives for honor and courage, and the appetitive soul pursues bodily desires. Aristotle, Plato's student, offered a different perspective, seeing the soul as the form or essence of a living being. For Aristotle, the soul is not separate from the body but rather its life-giving principle.

In religious contexts, the soul often carries profound significance. In Christianity, the soul is seen as eternal and destined for an afterlife in heaven or hell based on one's earthly deeds and faith. Hinduism and Buddhism both acknowledge the existence of the soul, though their interpretations diverge. Hinduism speaks of the atman, an individual soul that undergoes reincarnation until achieving moksha, or liberation. Buddhism, however, challenges the notion of a permanent soul, emphasizing anatta (no-self) and the transient nature of all things, including what might be considered the soul.

Contemporary scientific and philosophical debates continue to explore the nature of the soul. Materialists argue that consciousness and identity are products of brain activity, dismissing the notion of a non-physical soul. In contrast, dualists maintain that mental states and consciousness cannot be fully explained by physical processes alone, suggesting that there is more to human existence than mere biological mechanisms. Additionally, some theories in quantum physics and consciousness studies propose that consciousness might be a fundamental aspect of the universe, potentially offering new ways to understand the soul.

As we ponder the concept of the soul, several questions arise that challenge us to think deeply about our own beliefs and experiences:

- If the soul is immortal, what implications does this have for how we live our lives and perceive death?
- How do different cultural and religious beliefs about the soul influence our understanding of identity and morality?
- Can modern science provide insights into the existence or nature of the soul, or is it a purely philosophical and spiritual matter?
- If consciousness can exist independently of the physical body, what does this mean for our understanding of reality and human experience?

These questions invite us to reflect on the profound mysteries of existence, encouraging an ongoing exploration of what it truly means to possess a soul.

Did You Know?

- The term 'psychology' has been derived from the Greek word 'psyche' translating as 'breath, spirit, soul' and 'logia' corresponding to 'study of.'
- It takes about 66 days for an average individual to make something a daily habit.
- Studies say that individuals who could instinctively use sarcasm to tackle a frivolous question have healthy minds.
- Individuals who have a deep sense of guilt are better at identifying the emotions and concerns of the people around them.

- We can understand any messed up sentence as long as the last and first letters of words are in correct places. Such as this sentence.
- We're naturally second-minded because other people don't approve.
- Yawning to have someone else's yawn is a normal phenomenon, despite not feeling exhausted or asleep. One of the myths regarding its infectiousness is that people 'catch' it to express empathy.
- An average individual's mind wanders 30% of the time.
- Eye pupil rises to 45% when an individual looks at somebody they love.
- We often tend to break down knowledge into classes of 3-4 objects in them. The Indian phone number is 984-973-2543. Three blocks with 3-4 bits in each chunk.

"The soul is placed in the body like a rough diamond, and must be polished, or the luster of it will never appear." - Daniel Defoe"

"The soul is the same in all living creatures, although the body of each is different." - Hippocrates

14. What is Truth? Epistemology

The concept of truth is a fundamental question in the field of epistemology, the branch of philosophy concerned with knowledge, belief, and justification. Understanding what constitutes truth and how we can know it has preoccupied philosophers for centuries, leading to a variety of theories and perspectives.

One of the most well-known theories is the Correspondence Theory of Truth. This theory posits that a statement is true if it corresponds to a fact or reality. For example, the statement "The sky is blue" is true if, indeed, the sky is blue. This view emphasizes an objective reality that our statements and beliefs aim to accurately describe. Aristotle articulated this idea, suggesting that to say what is, is, and what is not, is not, is to speak the truth.

Contrasting with the Correspondence Theory is the Coherence Theory of Truth. This theory asserts that truth is a matter of coherence among a set of beliefs or propositions. A statement is true if it fits logically and consistently within a broader system of beliefs. For instance, mathematical truths are often considered true because they are coherent within the framework of mathematical rules and axioms. This theory is often associated with rationalist philosophers such as Spinoza and Leibniz.

Another significant perspective is the Pragmatic Theory of Truth, popularized by philosophers like Charles Sanders Peirce and William James. According to this view, truth is what works or what is useful in achieving desired outcomes. A belief is true if it proves to be effective or beneficial in practical application. For example, scientific theories are considered true if they consistently predict and explain phenomena, even if they are subject to change as new evidence arises.

In contemporary discussions, the Deflationary Theory of Truth challenges the need for a substantive theory of truth altogether. Advocates of this view, such as Willard Van Orman Quine and Paul Horwich, argue that the concept of truth is merely a linguistic convenience. To say that a statement is true is simply to assert the statement itself. For example, to say "It is true that snow is white" is no different than saying "Snow is white."

As we delve into the nature of truth, several questions emerge that provoke deeper reflection:

- Can there be a single, universal truth, or is truth always relative to different perspectives and contexts?
- How do our methods of inquiry and verification affect our understanding of what is true?
- Is it possible to attain absolute certainty in our knowledge, or must we always remain open to revision and doubt?
- What role do language, culture, and power dynamics play in shaping our conception of truth?

Hippocrates "Truth is the cry of all, but the game of the few." - George Berkeley

This quote by George Berkeley, an influential philosopher in the empiricist tradition, reflects on the complexity and sometimes elusive nature of truth. It suggests that while truth is universally sought after and valued, its interpretation and application can vary significantly among different individuals or groups, highlighting the subjective and contested nature of truth in philosophical discourse.

15. The Ethics of Genetic Engineering

The ethics of genetic engineering is a complex and multifaceted issue that raises profound questions about the nature of human life, the limits of scientific intervention, and the potential consequences for society. Genetic engineering involves the direct manipulation of an organism's genes using biotechnology, with applications ranging from agriculture to medicine. While the technology holds great promise for solving many of humanity's problems, it also presents significant ethical challenges.

One of the primary ethical concerns is the potential for unintended consequences. The complexity of genetic interactions means that altering one gene could have unforeseen effects on other genes or biological systems. This raises the question of whether we have sufficient understanding and control to safely engineer genes without causing harm. For example, genetically modified crops may lead to environmental issues, such as reduced biodiversity or the unintended spread of modified genes to wild populations.

In the realm of human genetic engineering, the stakes are even higher. The possibility of editing human embryos to prevent genetic disorders, known as germline engineering, could eliminate diseases like cystic fibrosis or Huntington's disease. However, this also raises concerns about "designer babies," where genetic traits such as intelligence, physical appearance, or even behavior could be selected according to parental preferences. This could exacerbate social inequalities and lead to new forms of discrimination, as those who can afford genetic enhancements may gain significant advantages over those who cannot.

Another ethical issue is the question of consent. Future generations will be affected by genetic modifications made today, but they cannot consent to these changes. This challenges the ethical principle of autonomy, which holds that individuals should have the right to make decisions about their own bodies. The long-term impacts of genetic engineering on individuals and society are difficult to predict, further complicating the issue of informed consent.

Furthermore, there are significant concerns about the potential misuse of genetic engineering. In the wrong hands, genetic technology could be used for harmful purposes, such as creating biological weapons or implementing eugenic policies aimed at eliminating certain populations deemed undesirable. The potential for abuse underscores the need for robust ethical guidelines and international regulations to ensure that genetic engineering is used responsibly and for the benefit of all.

1. **Glow-in-the-Dark Animals**: Scientists have successfully created glow-in-the-dark animals, such as pigs and rabbits, by inserting jellyfish genes that produce green fluorescent protein (GFP). These experiments, while primarily for research purposes, highlight the incredible possibilities of genetic engineering.
2. **CRISPR Breakthrough**: The CRISPR-Cas9 gene-editing technology has revolutionized genetic engineering by allowing precise, targeted changes to DNA. This groundbreaking tool is faster, cheaper, and more accurate than previous methods, opening up new possibilities for genetic research and therapy.
3. **Genetically Modified Babies**: In 2018, a Chinese scientist announced the birth of the world's first genetically modified babies, who were altered to be resistant to HIV. This controversial experiment sparked a global ethical debate and led to calls for stricter regulations on human genetic engineering.
4. **Resurrecting Extinct Species**: Genetic engineering is being explored as a way to bring extinct species back to life, a process known as de-extinction. Scientists are working on projects to revive species such as the woolly mammoth by editing the genes of closely related living species, like elephants.

16. Friedrich Nietzsche

Friedrich Nietzsche was a profound and influential German philosopher whose work has shaped modern thought in various fields, including philosophy, psychology, and literature. His life and ideas are best understood through his own words, which offer deep insights into his complex character and intellectual journey.

> *"I am not a man, I am dynamite."*

Born on October 15, 1844, in Röcken, Prussia, Nietzsche's early life was marked by intellectual precocity. He excelled in his studies, eventually becoming a professor of philology at the University of Basel at the age of 24. This quote reflects his self-perception as a revolutionary thinker, intent on challenging and transforming established norms and beliefs.

> *"God is dead. God remains dead. And we have killed him."*

This statement from Nietzsche's "The Gay Science" epitomizes his critique of religion and the decline of traditional values in modern society. Nietzsche believed that the Enlightenment had eroded the foundations of Christian morality, leaving a void that needed to be filled with new values. His declaration was not a celebration but a profound commentary on the existential crisis facing humanity.

"He who fights with monsters should be careful lest he thereby become a monster." Nietzsche's exploration of morality and human nature often delved into the darker aspects of existence. This quote from "Beyond Good and Evil" serves as a caution about the dangers of becoming what we oppose. Nietzsche himself struggled with these themes, as his work often placed him in opposition to the prevailing moral and cultural standards of his time.

"That which does not kill us makes us stronger." From "Twilight of the Idols,"

This quote encapsulates Nietzsche's philosophy of resilience and the transformative power of suffering. Throughout his life, Nietzsche faced considerable personal challenges, including chronic illness and isolation. His philosophy often emphasized the importance of embracing adversity as a means to personal growth and self-overcoming.

"To live is to suffer, to survive is to find some meaning in the suffering."

Nietzsche's later years were marked by profound isolation and mental decline. By 1889, he suffered a mental breakdown, possibly exacerbated by his syphilis, leading to his institutionalization. This quote underscores his lifelong quest to find meaning in life's inherent struggles, a theme central to his philosophy.

"I tell you: one must still have chaos in oneself to give birth to a dancing star."

Despite his personal suffering, Nietzsche's work is suffused with a call to creativity and the affirmation of life. This quote from "Thus Spoke Zarathustra" reflects his belief in the potential for individuals to create their own values and meaning in a world devoid of inherent purpose.

1. **Proto-Existentialist**: Nietzsche is often considered a precursor to existentialist thinkers like Jean-Paul Sartre and Albert Camus. His exploration of themes such as the absurdity of existence, the death of God, and the creation of personal meaning deeply influenced existentialism.
2. **Philologist to Philosopher**: Nietzsche initially made his mark as a classical philologist, focusing on ancient Greek literature and philosophy. His transition from philology to philosophy marked a significant shift in his intellectual trajectory, culminating in his profound philosophical contributions.
3. **Overlooked During Lifetime**: Despite his profound impact on future generations, Nietzsche was relatively unknown and unappreciated during his lifetime. It was only after his death that his work gained widespread recognition and acclaim.
4. **Eternal Recurrence**: Nietzsche proposed the idea of "eternal recurrence" — the notion that all events in life will repeat infinitely. This concept challenges individuals to live their lives as if their actions would recur eternally, thereby affirming their choices and existence.

Did you know?

Friedrich Nietzsche's iconic mustache, often depicted in historical photographs and artistic renditions, became so iconic that it influenced the art world beyond philosophy. In fact, it's believed that Salvador Dalí, the renowned surrealist painter, fashioned his own distinctive mustache in homage to Nietzsche's, considering it a symbol of intellectual prowess and rebellion against societal norms.

Nietzsche's philosophical ideas not only influenced existentialism but also found an unexpected echo in the world of literature. In Jorge Luis Borges' short story "The Garden of Forking Paths," the character Dr. Yu Tsun, faced with the concept of infinite possibilities and decisions, reflects a Nietzschean struggle with the burden of choice and the quest for personal meaning amidst chaos.

17. Who Was John Locke?

John Locke (1632–1704) was an English philosopher and physician, widely regarded as one of the most influential Enlightenment thinkers and often referred to as the "Father of Liberalism." His contributions to political theory, epistemology, and education laid the groundwork for modern democratic societies and influenced the development of Western philosophy. Locke's ideas about the nature of human knowledge, government, and personal identity have had a lasting impact on a wide range of academic disciplines.

Locke's most notable work, "An Essay Concerning Human Understanding," published in 1689, explored the nature and limits of human knowledge. In this seminal text, he argued against the existence of innate ideas, proposing instead that the mind at birth is a tabula rasa, or blank slate. According to Locke, all knowledge is derived from sensory experience and reflection. This empiricist approach contrasted sharply with the rationalist philosophies of thinkers like Descartes and laid the foundation for modern empiricism.

In the realm of political philosophy, Locke's "Two Treatises of Government" (1689) had a profound influence on the development of modern democratic thought. In the First Treatise, Locke refuted the notion of the divine right of kings, a prevalent belief at the time. In the Second Treatise, he presented his theory of natural rights, arguing that individuals possess inherent rights to life, liberty, and property. Locke asserted that the primary role of government is to protect these rights, and that political authority is derived from the consent of the governed. This concept became a cornerstone of the American and French revolutions and continues to underpin contemporary democratic ideologies.

Locke also made significant contributions to the philosophy of education. His work "Some Thoughts Concerning Education" (1693) emphasized the importance of practical learning and moral education.

Locke believed that education should develop a child's character and reasoning abilities, preparing them for a life of responsible citizenship. His ideas on education influenced subsequent educational theorists and continue to resonate in modern pedagogical practices.

Beyond his philosophical and political writings, Locke was also a practicing physician and a member of the Royal Society. His medical training and interest in the natural sciences informed his empirical approach to philosophy. Locke's diverse interests and intellectual pursuits reflected his belief in the power of reason and inquiry to advance human knowledge and improve society. Throughout his life, he corresponded with other prominent thinkers and engaged in the intellectual debates of his time, leaving a legacy that has endured for centuries.

Ten Facts About John Locke

1. **Influence on the U.S. Constitution**: Locke's ideas about government and natural rights significantly influenced the framers of the United States Constitution, particularly Thomas Jefferson, who drew heavily on Locke's concepts when writing the Declaration of Independence.
2. **Religious Tolerance**: Locke was a proponent of religious tolerance and argued for the separation of church and state. His "Letter Concerning Toleration" (1689) advocated for the protection of religious freedom, influencing later discussions on religious liberty.
3. **Political Exile**: Due to his political views and associations, Locke spent several years in exile in the Netherlands during the reign of King James II. He returned to England after the Glorious Revolution of 1688, which brought William of Orange to the throne.
4. **Medical Career**: Locke was trained as a physician and worked as a personal physician to Anthony Ashley Cooper,

the 1st Earl of Shaftesbury. His medical knowledge influenced his empirical approach to philosophy.

5. **Impact on Education**: Locke's educational theories emphasized the importance of nurturing a child's character and reasoning abilities. He advocated for learning through experience and practical engagement rather than rote memorization.
6. **Critique of Innate Ideas**: Locke's rejection of innate ideas was a direct challenge to the prevailing Cartesian philosophy. He argued that all human knowledge is derived from experience, a foundational concept in empiricism.
7. **Economic Thought**: Locke made contributions to economic theory, particularly in his writings on property and value. He argued that property rights are derived from labor and that the accumulation of wealth should be limited by the needs of others.
8. **Library and Collections**: Locke was an avid collector of books and manuscripts. His extensive library reflected his wide-ranging interests in philosophy, science, medicine, and politics.
9. **Correspondence with Newton**: Locke corresponded with Sir Isaac Newton, discussing topics such as religion and metaphysics. Their intellectual exchange highlights the interconnectedness of scientific and philosophical inquiry during the Enlightenment.
10. **Lasting Legacy**: Locke's works have been continuously studied and debated for over three centuries. His contributions to political theory, epistemology, and education continue to influence contemporary thought and are considered foundational texts in their respective fields.

18. The Philosophy of Time Travel

The concept of time travel has fascinated philosophers, scientists, and writers for centuries, posing profound questions about the nature of time, causality, and existence. At its core, time travel involves moving between different points in time, akin to how we move through space. This idea raises various philosophical theories and paradoxes that challenge our understanding of reality.

One prominent theory in the philosophy of time travel is the **Block Universe Theory**, which posits that past, present, and future all exist simultaneously in a four-dimensional spacetime block. According to this view, time is like a landscape that we traverse, and all events are fixed and unchangeable. This theory aligns with Albert Einstein's theory of relativity, suggesting that time is another dimension like space.

Another significant theory is the **Many-Worlds Interpretation**, often associated with quantum mechanics. This interpretation proposes that every possible outcome of a decision creates a new, parallel universe. In the context of time travel, this means that altering the past would create a divergent timeline, thus avoiding paradoxes like the Grandfather Paradox, where one could theoretically prevent their own existence.

The **Grandfather Paradox** itself presents a classic challenge to the possibility of time travel. If a time traveler were to go back and kill their grandfather before their parent was conceived, it would prevent the traveler's own birth, thus preventing the act of traveling back in time in the first place. This paradox raises questions about the consistency of timelines and whether the past can indeed be altered.

Compatibilism offers another perspective by reconciling free will with determinism in the context of time travel. Compatibilists argue that even if our actions are determined by prior events, we can still be considered free if we act according to our desires and intentions. This view allows for the possibility of time travel without undermining human agency, suggesting that while our choices may be predetermined, they are still ours to make.

1. **Time Dilation**: According to Einstein's theory of relativity, time passes differently for observers moving at different speeds. Astronauts on the International Space Station age slightly slower than people on Earth due to this phenomenon.
2. **Wormholes**: Theoretical physicists propose that wormholes could act as shortcuts through spacetime, potentially allowing for time travel. However, creating and stabilizing a wormhole remains purely speculative.
3. **Twin Paradox**: In relativity theory, the twin paradox describes a scenario where one twin travels at near-light speed while the other remains on Earth. Upon return, the traveling twin would be younger than their sibling due to time dilation.
4. **Novikov Self-Consistency Principle**: This principle suggests that any actions taken by a time traveler were always part of history, thereby preventing paradoxes. It implies that the timeline is self-consistent and unchangeable.
5. **Chronology Protection Conjecture**: Physicist Stephen Hawking proposed this conjecture, arguing that the laws of physics prevent time travel on macroscopic scales, thereby protecting the timeline from paradoxes.
6. **Closed Timelike Curves**: In general relativity, closed timelike curves are paths through spacetime that return to the same point in time and space, theoretically allowing for time travel.
7. **Quantum Time Travel**: Some interpretations of quantum mechanics propose that particles can influence past events

through quantum entanglement, potentially opening the door to time travel on a microscopic scale.
8. **Block Universe Theory**: This theory posits that past, present, and future all exist simultaneously in a four-dimensional spacetime block, suggesting that time travel could be possible within this framework.
9. **Faster-than-Light Travel**: If humans could travel faster than light, it could theoretically allow us to travel back in time, as suggested by special relativity. However, achieving such speeds remains beyond current technological capabilities.
10. **Retrocausality**: This concept in quantum physics suggests that future events can influence past events. Though highly theoretical, it opens up fascinating possibilities for time travel and causality.

"Time travel used to be thought of as just science fiction, but Einstein's general theory of relativity allows for the possibility that we could warp space-time so much that you could go off in a rocket and return before you set out."

- Stephen Hawking

This quote from Stephen Hawking encapsulates the intersection of theoretical physics and the philosophical implications of time travel, suggesting that our understanding of spacetime could potentially allow for such extraordinary feats.

19. The Paradox of the Barber

The Paradox of the Barber, also known as the Barber Paradox, is a self-referential puzzle that highlights the inconsistencies that can arise in formal systems of logic and set theory. It was formulated by the British philosopher and logician **Bertrand Russell** in the early 20th century as a way to illustrate problems related to self-reference and set membership.

The paradox is set in a hypothetical village where there is a single barber who shaves all and only those men in the village who do not shave themselves. The question then arises: does the barber shave himself? If the barber shaves himself, according to the definition, he must not shave himself because he only shaves those who do not shave themselves. Conversely, if the barber does not shave himself, then he must shave himself because he shaves all those who do not shave themselves. This creates a logical contradiction, making it impossible to determine whether the barber shaves himself or not.

This paradox illustrates a significant problem in set theory, particularly related to the concept of a set that contains itself as a member. Russell's Paradox, a more general form of this logical puzzle, demonstrates that certain sets, such as the set of all sets that do not contain themselves, lead to contradictions. This was a critical discovery in the foundations of mathematics, showing that naive set theory, which assumed any definable collection could form a set, was flawed.

To resolve these contradictions, mathematicians and logicians developed more rigorous frameworks for set theory. One such framework is Zermelo-Fraenkel set theory (ZF), which includes specific axioms to prevent such paradoxical sets. Another approach is to use type theory, where elements and sets are assigned to different types, preventing a set from containing itself as a member. These advancements helped to establish a more consistent and robust foundation for mathematics.

The Barber Paradox also has implications beyond mathematics, influencing philosophical discussions about self-reference, language, and logic. It serves as a cautionary tale about the limits of formal systems and the need for careful definitions and frameworks to avoid contradictions. The paradox encourages deeper reflection on how we define and categorize concepts, highlighting the delicate balance required to maintain logical consistency.

20. Karl Marx Through Quotes

Karl Marx, a revolutionary thinker and philosopher, profoundly influenced the course of modern history with his critique of capitalism and his vision of a classless society. Here, we explore his life and ideas through some of his most famous quotes, shedding light on his contributions to political theory, economics, and sociology.

"The history of all hitherto existing society is the history of class struggles."

From "The Communist Manifesto," this quote encapsulates Marx's central thesis that societal development is driven by conflicts between different social classes. He believed that these class struggles, particularly between the bourgeoisie (capitalist class) and the proletariat (working class), would ultimately lead to a revolutionary change and the establishment of a classless society.

"The philosophers have only interpreted the world, in various ways; the point, however, is to change it."

This quote from Marx's "Theses on Feuerbach" highlights his practical approach to philosophy. Unlike previous philosophers who focused on understanding and interpreting the world, Marx emphasized the importance of transforming it through revolutionary action. This perspective laid the foundation for his involvement in political activism and his call for the working class to rise against capitalist exploitation.

"Religion is the opium of the people."

In his critique of religion, found in "A Contribution to the Critique of Hegel's Philosophy of Right," Marx argued that religion serves as a tool of oppression, providing an illusory sense of happiness to the masses while distracting them from the harsh realities of their exploitation. He believed that by promising a better afterlife, religion pacified the working class and prevented them from seeking social and economic justice in their current lives.

"From each according to his ability, to each according to his needs."

This principle, outlined in Marx's "Critique of the Gotha Program," reflects his vision of a communist society where resources and wealth are distributed based on individuals' needs rather than their ability to pay. Marx argued that such a system would eliminate social inequalities and ensure that everyone has access to the necessities of life, fostering a sense of collective responsibility and cooperation.

"The mode of production of material life conditions the general process of social, political and intellectual life.

"In "A Contribution to the Critique of Political Economy," Marx asserts that the economic base of society—its mode of production—shapes all other aspects of life, including politics, culture, and ideology. This idea, known as historical materialism, suggests that changes in the economic structure lead to changes in the social superstructure, driving societal evolution.

- **Dialectical Materialism**: Marx developed the concept of dialectical materialism, which combines Hegelian dialectics with a materialist view of history. This framework posits that societal progress occurs through the resolution of contradictions within the material conditions of life.
- **Capital**: In his seminal work "Das Kapital," Marx provided a detailed analysis of the capitalist system, examining the dynamics of labor, production, and capital accumulation. He argued that capitalism inherently leads to the exploitation of workers and the concentration of wealth in the hands of a few.
- **Influence**: Marx's ideas have had a profound impact on various fields, including economics, sociology, and political science. His theories inspired numerous social movements and revolutions, most notably the Russian Revolution of 1917, which led to the establishment of the Soviet Union.
- **Collaborator**: Friedrich Engels, a close collaborator and friend of Marx, played a crucial role in developing and disseminating Marxist theory. Together, they authored "The Communist Manifesto" and worked on various other projects to promote their revolutionary ideas.
- **Legacy**: Despite the fall of many Marxist regimes in the late 20th century, Marx's critique of capitalism remains influential. His ideas continue to be studied and debated, offering insights into contemporary issues such as economic inequality, globalization, and workers' rights.

Communism, as envisioned by Karl Marx, aimed at creating a classless society where the means of production are collectively owned, and resources are distributed based on need. However, the practical implementations of communism in the 20th and 21st centuries have varied widely from Marx's theoretical framework. Below, we explore several examples of modern-day communism in practice, examining whether they adhered to or deviated from Marx's philosophical principles.

Soviet Union (1922-1991)

The Soviet Union, established after the Russian Revolution of 1917, was one of the earliest and most prominent attempts to implement Marxist principles. Under Lenin and later Stalin, the Soviet government nationalized industry and collectivized agriculture in an effort to eliminate private ownership. However, several deviations from Marx's vision emerged:

- **Totalitarianism**: Rather than a classless society, the Soviet Union developed a highly centralized, authoritarian regime. Political dissent was not tolerated, and the Communist Party maintained strict control over all aspects of life.
- **Economic Challenges**: While the Soviet economy initially experienced industrial growth, it eventually stagnated due to inefficiencies and lack of innovation. The planned economy struggled to meet the needs of its citizens, leading to shortages and poor living standards.

People's Republic of China (1949-Present)

After the Chinese Communist Party, led by Mao Zedong, gained control in 1949, China embarked on a series of socialist reforms. Key initiatives included land redistribution, collectivization, and the establishment of state-owned enterprises. Yet, significant deviations from Marxist principles occurred:

- **Cultural Revolution**: Mao's Cultural Revolution (1966-1976) aimed to eradicate "bourgeois" elements from society, resulting in widespread persecution and destruction of cultural heritage. This period deviated from Marx's emphasis on rational, economic development.
- **Economic Reforms**: Since the late 1970s, China has embraced market reforms under Deng Xiaoping, introducing

elements of capitalism within its socialist framework. While the state still controls key sectors, private enterprise and foreign investment have become integral to the economy, leading to significant economic growth but also increased inequality.

Cuba (1959-Present)

Cuba, under Fidel Castro, adopted a Marxist-Leninist model following the 1959 revolution. The Cuban government nationalized industries, implemented land reforms, and provided universal healthcare and education. However, challenges and deviations include:

- **Economic Isolation**: U.S. sanctions and the collapse of the Soviet Union severely impacted the Cuban economy, leading to shortages and economic hardship.
- **Human Rights Issues**: The Cuban government has been criticized for suppressing political dissent and restricting freedoms, diverging from the ideals of equality and freedom espoused by Marx.

Vietnam (1976-Present)

After the Vietnam War, North and South Vietnam were reunified under a communist government. The Vietnamese government pursued socialist economic policies, including collectivization and nationalization. However:

- **Doi Moi Reforms**: In 1986, Vietnam introduced Doi Moi (renovation) reforms, shifting towards a mixed economy with market-oriented policies while maintaining political control by the Communist Party. These reforms led to significant economic growth but also increased inequality.

Deviations and Challenges

- **Authoritarianism vs. Classlessness**: Many communist regimes have developed authoritarian structures, contrary to Marx's vision of a classless and stateless society.
- **Economic Inefficiencies**: Centralized planning and lack of market mechanisms often resulted in economic inefficiencies and stagnation.
- **Human Rights Violations**: The suppression of political dissent and restriction of freedoms are common features in many communist states, conflicting with the ideals of human emancipation and freedom that Marx advocated.

21. Understanding Phobias: Weird and Common Fears

Phobias are intense, irrational fears of specific objects, situations, or activities that pose little or no actual danger. They fall under the category of anxiety disorders and can significantly impact an individual's daily life. By exploring the nature of phobias, we can better understand their psychological roots, common types, and some of the more unusual fears that people experience.

Phobias are more than just everyday fears; they involve an overwhelming sense of dread and can trigger severe anxiety symptoms, including panic attacks. These responses are disproportionate to the actual threat posed by the feared object or situation. Phobias often develop during childhood or adolescence but can emerge at any age. The exact cause of phobias is not entirely understood, but they are believed to result from a combination of genetic predisposition, brain chemistry, and environmental factors.

Many phobias are widely recognized and understood due to their prevalence in the population. Some of the most common phobias include:

- **Arachnophobia**: Fear of spiders. This is one of the most widespread phobias and can cause extreme anxiety even when seeing a spider or thinking about one.
- **Acrophobia**: Fear of heights. People with acrophobia may experience vertigo, dizziness, and a sense of panic when in high places or even thinking about them.
- **Claustrophobia**: Fear of confined spaces. This phobia can make it difficult for individuals to use elevators, airplanes, or even small rooms.
- **Agoraphobia**: Fear of open or crowded spaces. This complex phobia can lead to avoidance of places or situations

where escape might be difficult, potentially confining individuals to their homes.
- **Social Phobia (Social Anxiety Disorder)**: Fear of social situations. Those with social phobia fear being judged or embarrassed in public, which can severely restrict their social interactions and activities.

Beyond the common fears, there are many less known and more unusual phobias that affect individuals. These phobias can be equally debilitating and often draw curiosity due to their uncommon nature:

- **Ablutophobia**: Fear of bathing or washing. Individuals with this phobia avoid activities related to cleanliness, which can lead to social and health issues.
- **Coulrophobia**: Fear of clowns. Despite clowns being intended as comedic figures, some people experience intense fear at the sight of them, often triggered by their exaggerated features and makeup.
- **Nomophobia**: Fear of being without a mobile phone or beyond mobile phone contact. This modern phobia reflects the increasing reliance on technology and the anxiety of being disconnected.
- **Xanthophobia**: Fear of the color yellow. People with this phobia avoid yellow objects, which can include everyday items like flowers, cars, or even clothing.
- **Turophobia**: Fear of cheese. This unusual phobia can cause individuals to feel extreme disgust or fear when in the presence of cheese, affecting their diet and social interactions.

Phobias often develop as a result of traumatic experiences, learned behaviors, or deep-seated psychological conflicts. The psychological mechanisms underlying phobias can include:

- **Classical Conditioning**: A traumatic event associated with a specific object or situation can condition an individual to fear

that object or situation in the future. For example, a child bitten by a dog may develop a lifelong fear of dogs.
- **Observational Learning**: Witnessing others display fear or anxiety towards an object or situation can lead to the development of similar fears. Children, in particular, are susceptible to adopting their parents' or peers' fears.
- **Biological Factors**: Genetic predisposition and brain chemistry can play a role in the development of phobias. Some individuals may have a heightened sensitivity to fear and anxiety, making them more prone to developing phobias.
- **Cognitive Factors**: Negative thought patterns and beliefs can exacerbate phobias. Individuals with phobias often overestimate the danger posed by their fears and underestimate their ability to cope.

Crazy Facts About Phobias

1. **Cultural Variations**: Phobias can vary significantly across cultures. For example, in Japan, "Taijin Kyofusho" is a social anxiety disorder characterized by the fear of offending others with one's appearance, body odor, or behavior.
2. **Phobia Therapy**: Virtual reality exposure therapy (VRET) is an emerging treatment for phobias that uses virtual reality technology to expose patients to their fears in a controlled environment, helping them to gradually overcome their anxiety.
3. **Phobia Names**: The names of phobias are often derived from Greek or Latin roots. For example, "Arachnophobia" comes from the Greek word "arachne" (spider) and "phobos" (fear).
4. **Evolutionary Roots**: Some researchers believe that certain common phobias, such as fear of snakes or spiders, have evolutionary roots. These fears may have developed to protect early humans from dangerous animals.

22. The Psychology Behind Screen Time

In our increasingly digital world, screen time has become a central part of daily life for people of all ages. From work and education to entertainment and social interaction, screens dominate our environment. Understanding the psychological effects of screen time is crucial as we navigate the benefits and potential drawbacks of our digital engagement.

Screen time encompasses the total amount of time spent on devices such as smartphones, tablets, computers, and televisions. Statistics highlight the extensive use of these devices:

- **Adults**: On average, adults spend about 11 hours per day interacting with media, including television, computers, and mobile devices.
- **Children and Adolescents**: According to the American Academy of Pediatrics, children aged 8-12 spend around 4-6 hours per day on screens, while teens can spend up to 9 hours per day.
- **Global Usage**: A 2019 report from Hootsuite and We Are Social found that the average internet user spends 6 hours and 42 minutes online daily.

Psychological Impacts of Screen Time

1. Cognitive Effects

- **Attention and Concentration**: Excessive screen time, especially involving fast-paced content like video games and social media, can impact attention spans. Studies suggest that

heavy screen use is associated with difficulties in focusing and sustaining attention, particularly in children.
- **Sleep Disruption**: Screen use before bedtime is linked to poor sleep quality. The blue light emitted by screens can interfere with the production of melatonin, a hormone that regulates sleep. This disruption can lead to insufficient sleep and its associated cognitive impairments, such as reduced memory and problem-solving abilities.

2. Mental Health

- **Anxiety and Depression**: High levels of screen time, particularly on social media, have been correlated with increased rates of anxiety and depression. This is attributed to factors such as cyberbullying, social comparison, and the pressure to maintain a perfect online persona.
- **Addiction**: Screen time can become addictive, especially in the context of video games and social media. The design of these platforms often includes features that trigger dopamine release in the brain, creating a reward cycle that can lead to compulsive use.

3. Physical Health

- **Sedentary Lifestyle**: Excessive screen time contributes to a sedentary lifestyle, which is associated with various health issues, including obesity, cardiovascular disease, and type 2 diabetes. The lack of physical activity can also negatively impact mental health and overall well-being.
- **Vision Problems**: Prolonged screen use can lead to digital eye strain, characterized by symptoms such as dry eyes, headaches, and blurred vision. The American Optometric Association recommends the 20-20-20 rule: taking a 20-second break to look at something 20 feet away every 20 minutes.

4. Social Effects

- **Reduced Face-to-Face Interaction**: Increased screen time can lead to a decline in face-to-face social interactions, which are crucial for developing and maintaining strong interpersonal relationships. This reduction in direct social contact can affect social skills and emotional intelligence.
- **Family Dynamics**: Screen time can impact family relationships, with less time spent on shared activities and meaningful conversations. Setting screen time boundaries and encouraging device-free time can help strengthen family bonds.

Stats and Research Findings

- **Children and Media Use**: The Kaiser Family Foundation reported that children aged 8-18 spend an average of 7 hours and 38 minutes using entertainment media across a typical day (more than 53 hours a week).
- **Sleep and Screens**: Research published in JAMA Pediatrics found that each additional hour of screen time was associated with 3-8 minutes less sleep per night.
- **Mental Health Correlation**: A study from the University of Pennsylvania found that limiting social media use to 30 minutes per day significantly reduced feelings of loneliness and depression over three weeks.
- **Productivity**: The Economist Intelligence Unit reported that 54% of employees find that technology has a positive impact on their productivity, while 42% believe it has a negative impact due to distractions and multitasking.

Here are some questions for you to ponder on?

- How does the increasing reliance on screens impact our cognitive development, particularly in children and adolescents?

- In what ways might prolonged screen time alter our social interactions and the quality of our relationships with family and friends?
- What are the potential long-term effects of screen-induced sleep disruption on our overall mental and physical health?
- How does the design of digital platforms, aimed at maximizing engagement, influence our behavior and potentially lead to addictive patterns of use?

"Technology can be our best friend, and technology can also be the biggest party pooper of our lives. It interrupts our own story, interrupts our ability to have a thought or a daydream, to imagine something wonderful, because we're too busy bridging the walk from the cafeteria back to the office on the cell phone."

— Steven Spielberg

This quote from Steven Spielberg touches on the dual nature of technology and screen time. While technology can enhance our lives and productivity, it also has the potential to interrupt personal reflection, creativity, and meaningful social interactions. It underscores the importance of balancing digital engagement with moments of unplugged time for deeper reflection and imagination.

23. Why Do We Dream? Theories and Interpretations

Dreams have fascinated humans for millennia, inspiring a wide array of philosophical beliefs and scientific inquiries. Throughout history, different cultures and thinkers have offered diverse interpretations of why we dream, each providing unique insights into the nature of the subconscious mind.

Philosophical Beliefs

Freudian Theory

Sigmund Freud, the father of psychoanalysis, proposed that dreams are a manifestation of our deepest unconscious desires and anxieties. According to Freud, dreams provide a safe outlet for repressed wishes and emotions. He believed that analyzing dreams could reveal hidden aspects of an individual's psyche, offering a window into their unconscious mind.

Jungian Theory

Carl Jung, a student of Freud, expanded on his mentor's ideas by introducing the concept of the collective unconscious. Jung suggested that dreams are not only personal but also draw from a shared reservoir of archetypes and symbols common to all humanity. For Jung, dreams play a crucial role in the process of individuation, helping individuals integrate different aspects of their personality and achieve psychological wholeness.

Philosophical Idealism

Philosophical idealists like George Berkeley posited that reality is fundamentally mental or spiritual in nature. Dreams, in this view, challenge our understanding of what is real, blurring the line between waking life and the dream world. Idealists often see dreams as symbolic narratives that offer insights into the nature of reality and the self.

Existentialist Perspective

Existentialists such as Jean-Paul Sartre and Martin Heidegger explored dreams as reflections of our existential concerns. Dreams can reveal our struggles with meaning, freedom, and the nature of existence. Existentialists might see dreams as a way to confront our authentic selves, revealing truths that we might avoid in our waking lives.

Scientific Theories

Activation-Synthesis Theory

Proposed by J. Allan Hobson and Robert McCarley, this theory suggests that dreams result from the brain's attempt to make sense of random neural activity during REM (rapid eye movement) sleep. According to this view, the brain synthesizes a coherent narrative from these random signals, leading to the experience of dreaming. Activation-synthesis theory posits that dreams may not have inherent meaning but are rather by-products of brain activity.

Cognitive Theories

Some cognitive scientists believe that dreaming plays a crucial role in memory consolidation, helping to process and integrate experiences from the waking day. This theory suggests that dreams help to strengthen important memories and discard irrelevant information. Another cognitive perspective is that dreams facilitate problem-solving by allowing the mind to work through complex issues in a creative and less constrained manner.

Threat Simulation Theory

Proposed by Antti Revonsuo, this theory argues that dreaming serves an evolutionary function by simulating threatening situations. This allows individuals to rehearse responses to potential dangers, thereby improving their chances of survival in real life. Dreams, in this context, are seen as an adaptive mechanism that enhances an individual's preparedness for real-world threats.

Neurobiological Theories

Some neurobiologists suggest that dreams help maintain and develop neural connections. During REM sleep, the brain may engage in maintenance activities that promote overall brain health and function. Another neurobiological perspective is that dreaming helps regulate emotions by processing emotional experiences and reducing stress.

Bridging Philosophy and Science

While philosophical beliefs and scientific theories offer different perspectives on why we dream, there are intriguing intersections between the two. For example, Freud's idea of dreams as expressions of unconscious desires finds some resonance in modern cognitive theories that explore the role of dreams in processing emotions and experiences. Similarly, Jung's concept of the collective unconscious parallels neurobiological theories that emphasize the shared, adaptive functions of dreaming.

Dreams remain a rich area of exploration, blending the insights of philosophy and science. Both fields continue to unravel the mysteries of the dreaming mind, offering a deeper understanding of the complexities of human consciousness and the functions of our nocturnal visions.

Did You Know?

- During REM sleep, your body experiences a form of temporary paralysis known as REM atonia, which prevents you from acting out your dreams. Occasionally, people wake up during this phase and experience a few moments of immobility, known as sleep paralysis.
- Some people experience a rare phenomenon called Exploding Head Syndrome, which involves hearing loud noises, like an explosion or gunshot, as they are falling asleep or waking up. Despite the startling sounds, it's completely harmless.
- Your brain can experience "microsleeps," which are brief, involuntary episodes of sleep that last only a few seconds, often occurring when a person is extremely sleep-deprived. During microsleeps, parts of the brain shut down even while you're still awake.
- Some people can control their dreams through a phenomenon known as lucid dreaming, which occurs when a person becomes aware that they are dreaming and can manipulate the dream's content. Techniques such as reality testing and keeping a dream journal can increase the likelihood of experiencing lucid dreams.
- Your brain consolidates memories and processes information while you sleep. During sleep, particularly REM sleep, the brain strengthens neural connections and reorganizes memories, enhancing learning and problem-solving skills.
- Sleepwalking, or somnambulism, usually occurs during deep non-REM sleep. Sleepwalkers can perform complex activities, such as walking, eating, or even driving, with no memory of the events upon waking. It's more common in children than adults.
- Being deprived of REM sleep, the stage in which most vivid dreaming occurs, can lead to increased irritability, anxiety, and difficulty concentrating. Over time, the brain will

compensate by increasing REM sleep in subsequent nights, a phenomenon known as REM rebound.
- People's sleep patterns are influenced by their chronotype, or natural inclination toward morning or evening activity. "Morning larks" prefer to wake up early and are most alert in the morning, while "night owls" feel more awake and productive later in the day and night.
- Adequate sleep is crucial for a healthy immune system. During sleep, the body produces cytokines, proteins that help fight infection and inflammation. Chronic sleep deprivation can weaken immune response, making you more susceptible to illness.
- The longest recorded period without sleep is 11 days. In 1964, 17-year-old Randy Gardner stayed awake for 264 hours as part of a science experiment. Despite experiencing significant cognitive and physical impairments, he recovered without long-term effects after returning to a normal sleep schedule.

24. The Influence of Birth Order on Personality

Ever heard old wives' tales like "the oldest is always the most responsible" or "the youngest is always the most spoiled"? These sayings have been around for generations, but is there any truth to them? Let's find out by exploring the influence of birth order on personality.

The Oldest Child: The Responsible Leader

Old Wives' Tale: The oldest child is always the most responsible and mature.

Reality: Research often supports the notion that firstborns tend to take on leadership roles and exhibit higher levels of responsibility. This is likely due to the expectations placed on them by their parents. As the first child, they often receive undivided attention and are given more responsibilities, which can foster a sense of duty and leadership.

- Firstborns are often described as reliable, conscientious, and achievement-oriented. They may also be more conservative and cautious compared to their younger siblings.
- Studies have shown that firstborns are more likely to pursue higher education and leadership positions. For instance, a significant number of U.S. presidents and Nobel laureates are firstborn children.

The Middle Child: The Peacemaker

Old Wives' Tale: The middle child is always the peacemaker and the most adaptable.

Reality: Middle children often develop strong negotiation and social skills as they navigate their position between the older and younger siblings. They may not receive as much attention as the oldest or youngest, which can make them more independent and resourceful.

- Middle children are often seen as peacemakers, adaptable, and sociable. They might also feel overlooked, which can drive them to seek attention outside the family.
- Research indicates that middle children may excel in interpersonal relationships and are often skilled at negotiation and compromise.

The Youngest Child: The Charming Free Spirit

Old Wives' Tale: The youngest child is always the most spoiled and charming.

Reality: The youngest child often benefits from the more relaxed parenting style that typically comes with experience. Parents may be less strict and more indulgent, which can result in the youngest child being more carefree and sociable.

- Youngest children are frequently described as outgoing, charming, and sometimes rebellious. They are often more willing to take risks and seek attention.
- Studies suggest that youngest children may be more creative and open to new experiences. They often bring a sense of humor and liveliness to the family dynamic.

The Only Child: The Little Adult

Old Wives' Tale: The only child is always spoiled and lonely.

Reality: Only children grow up without siblings, which means they don't have to compete for their parents' attention. This can result in higher self-esteem and strong intellectual development, but it can also lead to pressure to succeed.

- Only children are often described as mature for their age, self-sufficient, and diligent. They may also be more comfortable with adults than peers.
- Research shows that only children can be high achievers and may develop advanced language skills early on. They are often seen as more independent and self-motivated.

The Big Picture

While birth order can influence personality traits, it is important to remember that it is just one factor among many. Genetics, parenting style, family dynamics, socio-economic status, and cultural context all play significant roles in shaping an individual's personality. Additionally, the perceived effects of birth order can vary widely among different families and cultures.

In conclusion, while there is some evidence to support the old wives' tales about birth order and personality, the reality is much more nuanced. Each child's unique experiences and environment contribute to their development, making them who they are. So, while the oldest might often be the responsible leader, the middle child the adaptable peacemaker, the youngest the charming free spirit, and the only child the mature little adult, there are always exceptions to the rule

25. How the Placebo Effect Works

The placebo effect is a fascinating phenomenon where patients experience real improvements in their health after receiving a treatment that has no therapeutic effect. This effect demonstrates the powerful connection between the mind and body and how psychological factors can influence physical health.

The Mechanism of the Placebo Effect

The placebo effect occurs when an individual believes that they are receiving a genuine medical treatment, even though the treatment has no active ingredients. This belief can trigger a range of physiological responses in the body. For instance, the expectation of relief can lead to the release of endorphins, the body's natural painkillers, which can reduce pain. Additionally, the placebo effect can activate brain regions associated with mood and emotion, such as the prefrontal cortex and the amygdala, further contributing to the perception of improved health.

Psychological and Neurological Factors

Several psychological factors contribute to the placebo effect, including the patient's expectations, conditioning, and the doctor-patient relationship. When patients expect a treatment to work, their belief can enhance their perception of its efficacy. Conditioning, where a patient learns to associate a particular treatment with a positive outcome, can also play a significant role. The trust and rapport between a patient and their healthcare provider can further strengthen the placebo effect, as patients are more likely to believe in the treatment if they have confidence in their doctor.

Impact on Various Medical Conditions

The placebo effect has been observed in a wide range of medical conditions, from pain management and depression to Parkinson's disease and irritable bowel syndrome. In pain management, for example, studies have shown that placebos can produce pain relief comparable to that of some analgesics. In mental health, placebos can have a significant impact on symptoms of depression and anxiety, demonstrating the importance of psychological factors in these conditions. Even in neurological disorders like Parkinson's disease, placebos can lead to measurable changes in brain activity, highlighting the profound influence of the mind on the body.

Limitations and Ethical Considerations

Despite its potential benefits, the placebo effect also has limitations and raises ethical questions. Not all patients respond to placebos, and the effect can vary widely among individuals. Moreover, using placebos in clinical practice can be ethically problematic, as it involves deceiving patients about the nature of their treatment. This deception can undermine trust in the doctor-patient relationship and complicate informed consent. Therefore, while the placebo effect offers valuable insights into the mind-body connection, its use in medical practice must be carefully considered.

Interesting Studies on the Placebo Effect

Placebos and Pain Relief

A landmark study published in "The Lancet" demonstrated that placebos could provide significant pain relief in patients with chronic pain conditions. In this study, patients who believed they were receiving a powerful analgesic reported pain relief similar to those who actually received the medication. One fascinating aspect of this study was the role of the patient's mindset and expectations. When patients were given the placebo by a doctor who expressed strong confidence in the treatment's effectiveness, the placebo effect was significantly stronger. This finding underscores the importance of the doctor-patient relationship and the power of suggestion in enhancing the placebo response.

Placebos in Surgery

An eye-opening study involving patients with osteoarthritis of the knee found that those who underwent a placebo surgery (where only small incisions were made without any actual surgical procedure) reported improvements in pain and function comparable to those who underwent real surgery. The study, published in "The New England Journal of Medicine," revealed that the mere act of undergoing a surgical procedure, even without therapeutic intervention, could trigger substantial placebo effects. This study has profound implications for understanding how patients' expectations and the ritual of surgery contribute to perceived improvements, suggesting that the context and experience of treatment play critical roles in healing.

Placebo and Parkinson's Disease

A groundbreaking study published in "Nature Neuroscience" explored the placebo effect in patients with Parkinson's disease, a condition characterized by reduced dopamine production in the brain. Researchers found that patients who received a placebo treatment exhibited increased dopamine production, similar to the response seen with active medication. This study provided direct evidence of the neurobiological basis of the placebo effect, showing that the expectation of treatment can trigger real biochemical changes in the brain. This finding is particularly significant as it demonstrates that the mind's expectations can have tangible effects on neurological function, potentially informing new approaches to treatment.

Open-Label Placebos

One of the most intriguing developments in placebo research is the discovery that even when patients are aware they are taking a placebo, they can still experience significant health benefits. A study on patients with irritable bowel syndrome (IBS), published in "PLoS ONE," found that those who knowingly took placebos reported symptom relief. Researchers believe that the act of taking a pill and the associated ritual, along with positive expectations set by the medical context, can contribute to the placebo effect. This study challenges the traditional notion that deception is necessary for the placebo effect and opens up new possibilities for ethical and transparent use of placebos in clinical practice.

> *"The doctor-patient relationship is critical to the placebo effect." - Irving Kirsch*

Did you know?

The color of a placebo pill can influence its perceived effectiveness. Studies have shown that red or orange placebos are often perceived as more stimulating or effective, while blue or green placebos are perceived as more calming. This phenomenon underscores how visual cues and expectations can significantly impact the placebo response, highlighting the complex interplay between psychology and physiology in medical treatment.

26. Why Do We Have Déjà Vu?

Ever get the feeling that you have experienced something before, even though you know it's the first time? This uncanny sensation is known as déjà vu, a French term meaning "already seen." Déjà vu is a mysterious and fascinating phenomenon that has intrigued psychologists, philosophers, and neuroscientists alike. Let's explore this sensation from both psychological and philosophical perspectives and delve into the scientific explanations behind it.

Psychological Perspective

From a psychological standpoint, déjà vu is often considered a form of memory anomaly. One theory suggests that it occurs due to a mismatch in the brain's memory systems. When we encounter a new situation, our brain processes it in two ways: the familiarity system, which assesses how familiar the situation feels, and the recollection system, which retrieves specific details about the situation. Déjà vu might happen when there is a fleeting glitch in the brain, causing the familiarity system to fire without the corresponding recollection. This results in a strong sense of familiarity without a clear memory, creating the eerie feeling of having lived through the moment before.

Philosophical Perspective

Philosophers have long pondered the nature of déjà vu. Some, like Plato, might argue that it hints at the existence of a realm of eternal forms and that our souls have experienced these forms before birth. This ties into the idea of anamnesis, or the recollection of innate knowledge. More modern philosophical interpretations might consider déjà vu as an illustration of the fallibility of human perception and memory. It challenges our understanding of time and reality, suggesting that our experiences of the present are influenced by complex, often subconscious, cognitive processes.

Neurobiological Theories

Neuroscientists have proposed several theories to explain the neurobiological underpinnings of déjà vu. One prevalent theory is that déjà vu results from temporal lobe dysfunction, particularly in the hippocampus and surrounding regions involved in memory processing. This dysfunction can cause a brief overlap or synchronization error between short-term and long-term memory circuits, making a new experience feel familiar.

Dual Processing Theory

Another explanation is the dual processing theory, which posits that two cognitive processes, such as perception and memory retrieval, become temporarily out of sync. When the brain processes information, it does so through multiple pathways. If one pathway processes the information slightly faster than the other, the delayed pathway might interpret the new information as a memory, creating a sensation of familiarity.

Split Perception Theory

The split perception theory suggests that déjà vu occurs when the brain takes in the same information twice in quick succession. The first perception might be brief and not fully processed, while the second, more detailed perception happens immediately after. This can trick the brain into feeling that the second perception is a repeat experience, leading to déjà vu.

Hologram Theory

A more novel scientific hypothesis is the hologram theory, which posits that memories are stored in the brain as holograms. When we encounter a situation that resembles a fragment of a past experience, the brain retrieves the entire memory hologram, giving the impression that the current moment has already occurred. This theory aligns with the idea that even a partial similarity between current and past experiences can trigger a full-blown déjà vu experience.

Intriguing Studies on Déjà Vu

1. Temporal Lobe Epilepsy

Research has shown that individuals with temporal lobe epilepsy frequently report experiencing déjà vu during seizures. This has led scientists to study the temporal lobe's role in memory and perception, providing insights into how brain activity can lead to the sensation of déjà vu.

2. Virtual Reality Experiments

In a study published in the journal "Psychological Science," researchers used virtual reality to recreate environments that induced déjà vu in participants. By subtly altering virtual scenes to resemble previous ones, they could artificially trigger the feeling of déjà vu, demonstrating how environmental similarities can lead to this phenomenon.

3. Eye-Tracking Studies

Eye-tracking technology has been used to investigate the visual patterns associated with déjà vu. Studies have found that when people experience déjà vu, their eye movements and visual attention patterns are similar to those seen when they correctly recognize something familiar, supporting the idea that déjà vu involves a misfiring of the brain's familiarity recognition system.

Common Triggers of Déjà Vu

1. Environmental Similarities

Being in a place that resembles a location you have previously visited, even if only slightly, can trigger déjà vu. The brain recognizes the similarities and mistakenly attributes them to a past experience.

2. Stress and Fatigue

High levels of stress or fatigue can make the brain more prone to memory processing errors, increasing the likelihood of experiencing déjà vu.

3. Routine Activities

Engaging in routine activities in new or slightly altered contexts can also trigger déjà vu. For example, visiting a new café that has a similar layout to one you frequently visit might cause a sense of familiarity.

Déjà vu remains a captivating subject of study that bridges the gap between psychology, philosophy, and neuroscience. While we have made significant strides in understanding its underlying mechanisms, it continues to challenge our perceptions of memory and reality, reminding us of the intricate complexities of the human mind.

Did you know?

Déjà vu tends to occur more frequently in younger adults, with studies suggesting that it peaks in individuals aged 15-25 years old. This age group experiences déjà vu more often than children or older adults, likely due to differences in brain development and cognitive processing during this stage of life.

27. The Concept of Infinity - A Philosophical Exploration

Infinity, an abstract and often perplexing concept, has intrigued philosophers, mathematicians, and thinkers for centuries. Philosophically, infinity challenges our understanding of the universe, existence, and the nature of reality. It pushes the boundaries of human comprehension, prompting deep reflections on the nature of the infinite.

Philosophical Perspectives on Infinity

Philosophically, infinity is often discussed in the context of time, space, and existence. Aristotle distinguished between potential infinity, a process that could continue indefinitely, and actual infinity, a completed set containing an infinite number of elements. "Actual infinity exists only in abstract concepts and cannot be realized in the physical world," he argued. This distinction has influenced subsequent philosophical debates, including those by Immanuel Kant, who contended that the human mind cannot fully grasp the concept of an infinite series.

Mathematical Infinity and Philosophical Implications

Mathematics provides a structured way to approach infinity, notably through the work of Georg Cantor. Cantor's theory of sets and his introduction of different sizes of infinity revolutionized mathematics and had profound philosophical implications. Cantor stated, "The essence of mathematics is its freedom," reflecting on the abstract yet fundamental nature of infinity. His work showed that not all infinities are equal, suggesting a complexity within infinity itself that mirrors philosophical inquiries into the nature of existence and reality.

> *"The essence of mathematics is its freedom." - Georg Cantor*

Infinity in Metaphysics and Cosmology

In metaphysics, infinity often relates to the nature of the universe and the concept of the eternal. Philosophers like Baruch Spinoza and Gottfried Wilhelm Leibniz posited that the universe itself is infinite. Spinoza's notion of God as an infinite substance encapsulating everything highlights a metaphysical approach to infinity, suggesting that everything finite is part of an infinite whole. Leibniz, on the other hand, introduced the idea of "the best of all possible worlds," implying an infinite array of possibilities governed by a pre-established harmony.

Existential and Ethical Considerations

Existential philosophers have also grappled with the concept of infinity. Jean-Paul Sartre and Albert Camus explored the idea of an infinite universe devoid of inherent meaning, posing existential questions about human purpose and freedom. Sartre famously said, "Man is condemned to be free; because once thrown into the world, he is responsible for everything he does." This statement reflects the overwhelming nature of infinite possibilities and the existential burden it places on individuals. Ethical considerations also emerge, as the infinite nature of human actions and their consequences challenge traditional moral frameworks.

> *"Actual infinity exists only in abstract concepts and cannot be*

realized in the physical world." - Aristotle

Crazy Facts About Infinity

1. **Hilbert's Hotel Paradox**: The paradox, proposed by mathematician David Hilbert, illustrates the strange properties of infinity. Imagine a hotel with an infinite number of rooms, all occupied. If a new guest arrives, they can still be accommodated by moving each existing guest to the next room, demonstrating that infinity plus one is still infinity.
2. **Infinite Monkey Theorem**: This theorem states that a monkey randomly hitting keys on a typewriter for an infinite amount of time will eventually type out the complete works of Shakespeare. It underscores the counterintuitive and often mind-boggling nature of infinity.
3. **Zeno's Paradoxes**: Ancient philosopher Zeno of Elea proposed paradoxes that challenge the concept of motion and infinity. One famous paradox suggests that Achilles can never catch up to a tortoise with a head start, as he must first reach the point where the tortoise was, by which time the tortoise has moved further ahead, and so on ad infinitum.
4. **Cantor's Diagonal Argument**: Georg Cantor's diagonal argument demonstrates that the set of real numbers is uncountably infinite, meaning its size is greater than that of the set of natural numbers. This distinction between different types of infinity is a cornerstone of modern set theory.
5. **Infinite Universes in Cosmology**: Some theories in cosmology propose the existence of an infinite number of parallel universes or a multiverse. This idea suggests that every possible outcome of every event exists in its own separate universe, pushing the concept of infinity to its limits and beyond.

28. The Psychology of Lying and Deception

Lying and deception are complex behaviors that have intrigued psychologists for decades. Understanding the psychological mechanisms behind why people lie, how they deceive others, and the impact of these behaviors on individuals and society is crucial. This exploration delves into the multifaceted nature of lying and deception, examining the motivations, types, detection, and consequences.

Motivations Behind Lying

People lie for a variety of reasons, ranging from self-preservation to social convenience. One primary motivation is to avoid punishment or negative consequences. For instance, a child might lie about breaking a vase to avoid scolding. Adults, on the other hand, might lie to avoid social embarrassment or professional repercussions. Another significant motivation is to gain advantage or personal benefit. This includes exaggerating qualifications on a resume or lying about one's achievements to enhance social status. Altruistic lying, where individuals lie to protect someone else's feelings or well-being, also plays a role in social interactions.

Types of Lies

Lies can be categorized into several types based on their purpose and nature. **White lies** are minor and often told to avoid hurting someone's feelings, such as complimenting a friend's unflattering haircut. **Blatant lies** are outright falsehoods that are easy to detect but are used with the hope that they will be believed due to their audacity. **Exaggerations** involve overstating facts or embellishing stories to make them more appealing or impressive. **Omissions**, where crucial information is withheld, are also a form of deception. Each type of lie serves different psychological and social functions, impacting relationships and trust.

The Mechanisms of Deception

Deception involves more than just verbal lies; it can include nonverbal cues and behaviors designed to mislead. Research indicates that when people lie, they often exhibit subtle physical signs such as increased blinking, fidgeting, or changes in voice pitch. These nonverbal cues are part of what psychologists call "leakage," where hidden emotions are inadvertently revealed through body language. Cognitive load theory suggests that lying requires more mental effort than telling the truth because it involves creating and maintaining a false narrative. This additional cognitive load can lead to inconsistencies in the liar's story and increased physiological arousal, which can sometimes be detected through lie detection methods like polygraphs.

Detecting Lies

Detecting deception is notoriously challenging, even for trained professionals. Polygraph tests, which measure physiological responses such as heart rate, blood pressure, and galvanic skin response, are commonly used but have limitations and are not infallible. Behavioral analysis and microexpression detection, as popularized by psychologist Paul Ekman, focus on fleeting facial expressions that may reveal genuine emotions inconsistent with the verbal message. While these methods can improve lie detection accuracy, they are not foolproof. Most people, including law enforcement officers, perform only slightly better than chance when trying to identify lies, highlighting the need for caution and multiple approaches in lie detection.

The Consequences of Lying

Lying can have profound psychological and social consequences. On an individual level, habitual lying can lead to increased stress, anxiety, and guilt, contributing to a cycle of further deception and psychological distress. In relationships, lying erodes trust and can lead to significant conflicts and breakdowns in communication. Chronic dishonesty can also affect an individual's reputation and lead to long-term consequences in personal and professional spheres. Societally, widespread deception can undermine social cohesion and trust in institutions, contributing to a culture of skepticism and cynicism.

The Ethics of Lying

The ethics of lying is a contentious area in philosophy and psychology. While some lies, such as those told to protect someone's feelings or safety, can be ethically justified, others, like deceit for personal gain, are widely condemned. Immanuel Kant famously argued that lying is always morally wrong, as it undermines the foundation of trust necessary for social cooperation. Conversely, utilitarian perspectives might justify lying if it results in greater overall happiness or well-being. Understanding the ethical dimensions of lying involves balancing the potential benefits and harms and considering the broader context in which the lie is told.

- **Polygraph Limitations**: Despite their widespread use, polygraph tests are not infallible. Studies suggest they are only about 70-90% accurate, as they measure physiological arousal, which can be influenced by factors other than lying, such as anxiety or fear.
- **Children and Lying**: Research shows that children begin to lie as early as age two. This early development of lying is linked to cognitive growth, indicating that the ability to lie is a sign of developing theory of mind and social intelligence.

- **Pathological Liars**: Pathological liars, also known as compulsive liars, often lie out of habit and without clear benefit. This behavior is sometimes linked to underlying psychological conditions such as personality disorders, including antisocial personality disorder.
- **Microexpressions**: Microexpressions are involuntary facial expressions that occur within a fraction of a second and reveal true emotions. Training in detecting these expressions can improve one's ability to spot deception, although it requires significant skill and practice.
- **Digital Deception**: With the rise of digital communication, new forms of lying have emerged, such as catfishing (creating fake online identities) and online impersonation. These digital deceptions can have serious emotional and financial consequences for victims.
- **Self-Deception**: Interestingly, people can also deceive themselves. Self-deception involves convincing oneself of a truth or reality that is false or only partially true. This can serve as a psychological defense mechanism to protect against uncomfortable truths or to maintain self-esteem.

Questions to Ask Yourself About Lying and Deception

Reflecting on your own behavior regarding lying and deception can be an enlightening and eye-opening exercise. Here are some questions to ponder:

- How many lies do you tell on average each day?
- How many of these lies are white lies?
- How many blatant lies do you tell?
- How often do you think you get caught lying?
- How do you feel after lying?
- Are there patterns in your lying behavior?
- How do you justify your lies to yourself?
- Would you prefer to live in a world where everyone told the truth?

29. The Ethics of Surveillance and Privacy: The Edward Snowden Case

The balance between surveillance for security and the right to privacy has been a contentious issue for years. This debate reached a fever pitch in 2013 when Edward Snowden, a former contractor for the National Security Agency (NSA), leaked classified information revealing the extent of government surveillance programs. This case has become a focal point for discussions on the ethics of surveillance and privacy.

The Snowden Revelations

Edward Snowden's disclosures revealed that the NSA was conducting extensive and largely unchecked surveillance on both American citizens and foreign nationals. Programs like PRISM allowed the NSA to collect vast amounts of data from major internet companies, including emails, chat logs, and other private communications. Additionally, metadata from phone calls was being collected indiscriminately, leading to widespread concerns about privacy and government overreach.

Snowden justified his actions by claiming that the public had a right to know about the government's actions, which he saw as a gross violation of privacy and civil liberties. He argued that the extent of the surveillance was not only illegal but also unconstitutional, infringing on the Fourth Amendment's protection against unreasonable searches and seizures.

Ethical Considerations

One of the central ethical questions raised by the Snowden case is the balance between national security and individual privacy. Proponents of the surveillance programs argue that they are essential tools for preventing terrorism and ensuring national security. They claim that in a post-9/11 world, such measures are necessary to protect citizens from potential threats.

Opponents, however, argue that these surveillance practices constitute a severe violation of privacy rights. They contend that the mass collection of data without individualized suspicion or judicial oversight is a dangerous precedent that undermines democratic values and personal freedoms. As Benjamin Franklin famously said, "Those who would give up essential liberty to purchase a little temporary safety deserve neither liberty nor safety."

Another significant ethical issue is the lack of transparency and accountability in the surveillance programs. The Snowden revelations highlighted how much of the surveillance was conducted without public knowledge or consent, raising questions about the democratic oversight of intelligence agencies. The secretive nature of these programs makes it difficult to hold those in power accountable and to ensure that they do not abuse their authority.

In a democratic society, transparency and accountability are crucial. Citizens must be informed about government actions that affect their rights and freedoms, and there must be mechanisms in place to hold officials accountable for any abuses of power. The Snowden case underscores the need for greater oversight and transparency in intelligence operations.

Whistleblowing and Morality

The ethics of Snowden's actions themselves are also subject to debate. Whistleblowing involves the disclosure of information that the whistleblower believes to be in the public interest. Snowden viewed his leaks as a moral obligation to expose wrongdoing and protect civil liberties. He argued that the potential harm caused by the surveillance programs outweighed the consequences of his actions.

Critics, however, view Snowden's leaks as a betrayal of trust and a threat to national security. They argue that his disclosures compromised intelligence operations and endangered lives by revealing sensitive information to potential adversaries. This raises the question of whether the moral duty to expose government misconduct can justify the potential risks to national security.

Impact on Society

The Snowden revelations have had a profound impact on society, sparking a global debate on surveillance and privacy. They have led to legal and policy changes, including the USA Freedom Act, which aimed to limit the NSA's ability to collect bulk phone data. The case has also increased public awareness of digital privacy issues and the importance of protecting personal information in an increasingly interconnected world.

Interesting Facts About the Snowden Case

1. **Global Reaction**: Snowden's leaks prompted international reactions, with some countries condemning the US surveillance programs and others reevaluating their own intelligence practices. His actions have had a lasting impact on global surveillance policies and diplomatic relations.
2. **Asylum in Russia**: After leaking the classified information, Snowden initially fled to Hong Kong before seeking asylum in Russia. He has remained in Russia since 2013, where he continues to advocate for privacy and digital rights.
3. **Media Impact**: The Snowden leaks were first published by journalists Glenn Greenwald and Laura Poitras. The ensuing

media coverage won several awards, including the Pulitzer Prize for Public Service, highlighting the crucial role of journalism in holding power to account.
4. **Public Opinion**: Public opinion on Snowden is deeply divided. Some view him as a hero who exposed government overreach and protected civil liberties, while others see him as a traitor who jeopardized national security.
5. **Technological Changes**: The revelations have spurred changes in how tech companies handle user data. Many companies have since implemented stronger encryption methods and pushed back against government demands for user information to protect customer privacy.
6. **Legal Repercussions**: In the wake of Snowden's disclosures, several legal challenges were filed against the NSA's surveillance programs. These cases have led to significant court rulings on the legality and constitutionality of mass data collection.

Did you know?

Edward Snowden's revelations sparked significant changes in global perceptions of surveillance. According to a Pew Research Center survey conducted in 2013, 56% of Americans believed that monitoring of U.S. citizens' phone calls and emails by the government was unacceptable, up from 52% in 2006 before Snowden's leaks. His actions fundamentally shifted public discourse on privacy and governmental oversight worldwide.

"Those who would give up essential liberty to purchase a little temporary safety deserve neither liberty nor safety."

- Benjamin Franklin

30. Who Was Immanuel Kant

Immanuel Kant was a German philosopher who is widely considered one of the most influential figures in Western philosophy. Born on April 22, 1724, in Königsberg, Prussia (now Kaliningrad, Russia), Kant's work fundamentally shaped modern philosophy, particularly in the realms of epistemology, ethics, and metaphysics. His rigorous approach to philosophy and his profound contributions have left a lasting legacy that continues to be studied and debated today.

Kant was born into a modest family, with his father working as a harness maker. Despite financial constraints, Kant's parents valued education and enrolled him in the Collegium Fridericianum, a Pietist school that emphasized religious devotion and academic rigor. In 1740, Kant entered the University of Königsberg, initially studying theology before shifting his focus to philosophy, mathematics, and the natural sciences. Influenced by the works of Leibniz and Newton, Kant developed a keen interest in the nature of knowledge and the physical world.

After completing his studies, Kant spent several years as a private tutor before securing a position as a lecturer at the University of Königsberg in 1755. Over the next few decades, he published a series of works that established his reputation as a formidable philosopher. However, it was not until the publication of "Critique of Pure Reason" in 1781 that Kant's philosophical genius was fully recognized. This seminal work sought to address the limitations and capabilities of human knowledge, proposing that while we can know the phenomena presented to us by our senses, the noumena, or things-in-themselves, remain inaccessible.

Kant's epistemological contributions are perhaps best encapsulated in his doctrine of transcendental idealism. He argued that human experience is shaped by the mind's inherent structures, such as space, time, and causality. According to Kant, these categories are not derived from experience but rather shape our perceptions, making knowledge possible. This groundbreaking perspective bridged the gap between rationalism and empiricism, asserting that while knowledge begins with experience, it is not entirely derived from it.

In addition to his work in epistemology, Kant made significant contributions to ethics, particularly with his concept of the categorical imperative. Presented in his work "Groundwork of the Metaphysics of Morals" (1785), the categorical imperative is a universal moral law that applies to all rational beings. Kant posited that moral actions are those performed out of duty and guided by principles that could be universally applied. This deontological approach contrasts with utilitarianism, focusing on the inherent morality of actions rather than their consequences.

Kant's later works, including the "Critique of Practical Reason" (1788) and the "Critique of Judgment" (1790), further explored metaphysics and aesthetics. In the "Critique of Judgment," Kant examined the nature of beauty and the sublime, proposing that aesthetic judgments are based on a harmonious relationship between the faculties of imagination and understanding. This work laid the foundation for subsequent developments in aesthetics and the philosophy of art.

Immanuel Kant's influence extends far beyond his own time, shaping various philosophical movements, including German Idealism, phenomenology, and existentialism. His insistence on the limits of human knowledge and the importance of moral duty has had a profound impact on both theoretical and practical philosophy. Kant's ideas continue to be central to contemporary debates in philosophy, demonstrating the enduring relevance of his work.

Interesting Facts About Immanuel Kant

1. **Routine and Discipline**: Kant was known for his highly disciplined and routine lifestyle. He reportedly adhered to a strict daily schedule, which included a precise time for

walking around Königsberg, so much so that the locals would set their clocks by his daily walks.
2. **Never Married**: Despite his many contributions to philosophy, Kant never married. He was deeply dedicated to his academic work and lived a relatively solitary life, with few close relationships outside of his intellectual circle.
3. **Influence on Modern Science**: Kant's work on the nature of space and time influenced not only philosophy but also the development of modern physics. His ideas about the subjective nature of time and space can be seen as precursors to some of the concepts later explored in the theory of relativity.
4. **Philosophical Shift**: Kant underwent a significant philosophical shift in his thinking, known as the "Copernican Revolution" in philosophy. This shift involved moving from the idea that knowledge conforms to objects to the revolutionary idea that objects conform to our knowledge, fundamentally changing the way we understand the relationship between the mind and the world.

"Thoughts without content are empty, intuitions without concepts are blind."

- Immanuel Kant

This quote encapsulates Kant's perspective that our knowledge and understanding of the world are shaped not only by our sensory experiences ("intuitions") but also by our conceptual framework ("concepts"). It highlights Kant's assertion that our mental faculties actively structure our perception of reality, rather than passively receiving it as it is. This philosophical insight marks a significant departure from earlier views that assumed the mind simply mirrors the external world.

31. Ancient Greek Philosophers Quiz

1. Who is considered the "Father of Western Philosophy"?

    a) Plato
    b) Socrates
    c) Aristotle
    d) Pythagoras

2. Which philosopher founded the Academy in Athens, one of the earliest institutions of higher learning in the Western world?

    a) Socrates
    b) Plato
    c) Aristotle
    d) Epicurus

3. Who was the student of Plato and the teacher of Alexander the Great?

    a) Socrates
    b) Pythagoras
    c) Zeno of Citium
    d) Aristotle

4. Which philosopher is known for the famous quote "The unexamined life is not worth living"?

    a) Socrates
    b) Plato
    c) Aristotle
    d) Heraclitus

5. Who wrote "The Republic," a Socratic dialogue concerning justice and the ideal state?

   a) Aristotle
   b) Plato
   c) Socrates
   d) Xenophon

6. Which philosopher is known for his theory of Forms or Ideas?

   a) Aristotle
   b) Parmenides
   c) Plato
   d) Socrates

7. Who is credited with founding the philosophical school of Stoicism?

   a) Epicurus
   b) Zeno of Citium
   c) Diogenes
   d) Heraclitus

8. Which pre-Socratic philosopher is famous for his assertion that "You cannot step into the same river twice"?

   a) Parmenides
   b) Heraclitus
   c) Thales
   d) Anaximander

9. Who is known for the Pythagorean theorem, which relates to the lengths of the sides of right-angled triangles?

   a) Socrates
   b) Plato
   c) Pythagoras
   d) Aristotle

10. Which philosopher's school taught that pleasure is the highest good, known as Epicureanism?

   a) Zeno of Citium
   b) Epicurus
   c) Diogenes
   d) Parmenides

Answers

1. b) Socrates

- Socrates did not leave behind any written works; his ideas and philosophies are known through the writings of his students, mainly Plato and Xenophon. His method of teaching, known as the Socratic method, involves asking a series of questions to stimulate critical thinking and illuminate ideas.

2. b) Plato

- Plato's Academy was founded around 387 BCE. It is considered one of the first institutions of higher learning in the Western world and lasted for several centuries, closing in 529 CE by order of the Byzantine emperor Justinian I.

3. d) Aristotle

- Aristotle's influence extends beyond philosophy to various fields, including biology, physics, and political theory. His works include "Nicomachean Ethics," "Politics," and "Metaphysics," which continue to be essential reading in philosophy.

4. a) Socrates

- Socrates was tried and executed in 399 BCE for corrupting the youth of Athens and impiety. His method of elenchus, or cross-examination, was aimed at revealing contradictions in his interlocutors' beliefs and leading them to a deeper understanding.

5. b) Plato

- "The Republic" explores justice, the just individual, and the just city-state. It introduces the allegory of the cave, which illustrates Plato's theory of Forms and the philosopher's journey from ignorance to knowledge.

6. c) Plato

- Plato's theory of Forms posits that the material world is only a shadow of the true reality, which consists of unchanging, perfect Forms or Ideas. This theory significantly influenced subsequent philosophical thought.

7. b) Zeno of Citium

- Zeno founded the Stoic school of philosophy around 300 BCE in Athens. Stoicism teaches the development of self-control and fortitude as a means of overcoming destructive emotions, emphasizing rationality and the natural order.

8. b) Heraclitus

- Heraclitus is known for his doctrine that change is central to the universe, encapsulated in the phrase "panta rhei" (everything flows). He believed that the constant state of flux is a fundamental characteristic of the cosmos.

9. c) Pythagoras

- Pythagoras founded a religious movement known as Pythagoreanism, which combined aspects of philosophy, religion, and mathematics. His followers believed in the transmigration of souls and the mystical significance of numbers.

10. b) Epicurus

- Epicurus founded his school, The Garden, in Athens around 306 BCE. Epicureanism teaches that pleasure, particularly mental pleasure, is the greatest good, but it also advocates for simple living and the avoidance of pain and fear, especially the fear of gods and death.

32. The Concept of Justice: A Philosophical Fact File

Ancient Philosophies of Justice

Plato (428/427 – 348/347 BCE)

Plato's concept of justice is deeply rooted in his philosophical works, particularly "The Republic." In this dialogue, Plato, through the character of Socrates, defines justice as a harmonious structure where everyone plays their appropriate role. For Plato, justice in an individual mirrors justice in the state, where each part functions optimally according to its nature. He believed that justice involves the proper alignment of the three parts of the soul: reason, spirit, and appetite, paralleling the three classes of society: rulers, auxiliaries, and producers. Justice, for Plato, is achieved when these parts perform their functions without interfering with each other.

> *"Justice means minding your own business and not meddling with other men's concerns."*

Aristotle (384 – 322 BCE)

Aristotle, a student of Plato, offered a different perspective on justice in his work "Nicomachean Ethics." He distinguished between two types of justice: distributive and corrective. Distributive justice concerns the fair allocation of resources within a community, based on merit, need, or other criteria. Corrective justice deals with rectifying wrongs, ensuring that equals are treated equally and unequals unequally, proportionate to their relevant differences. Aristotle's conception of justice emphasizes balance and proportionality, aiming to restore equilibrium when it is disrupted.

> *"The virtue of justice consists in moderation, as regulated by wisdom." - Nicomachean Ethics*

Medieval Philosophies of Justice

St. Augustine (354 – 430 CE)

St. Augustine integrated Christian theology with Platonic thought, exploring justice in the context of divine order. In "The City of God," Augustine contrasts the Earthly City, characterized by self-love and injustice, with the Heavenly City, marked by the love of God and true justice. He believed that true justice is unattainable in the earthly realm but is perfectly realized in the divine order of God. For Augustine, human justice should strive to reflect divine justice as closely as possible, promoting peace and order according to God's will.

St. Thomas Aquinas (1225 – 1274 CE)

Building on Aristotle, Aquinas developed a comprehensive theory of justice in his work "Summa Theologica." He categorized justice as a cardinal virtue and identified it as a habit whereby a person consistently wills to give each their due. Aquinas emphasized natural law, suggesting that justice is rooted in the natural order established by God. His concept of justice encompasses both legal justice (concerning the common good) and particular justice (relating to individual relationships), highlighting the importance of reason and divine law in achieving a just society.

Modern Philosophies of Justice

John Locke (1632 – 1704)

John Locke's theory of justice is grounded in his ideas about natural rights and the social contract. In "Two Treatises of Government," Locke argues that justice involves the protection of life, liberty, and property. He believed that individuals possess natural rights given by God, and the role of government is to protect these rights. For Locke, a just government is one that operates with the consent of the governed and upholds the principles of fairness and equality under the law.

Immanuel Kant (1724 – 1804)

Immanuel Kant's deontological approach to justice is based on the concept of duty and the categorical imperative. In his work "Groundwork for the Metaphysics of Morals," Kant posits that justice requires individuals to act according to universal moral laws that respect the autonomy and dignity of every person. He emphasizes that justice is not about achieving particular outcomes but about adhering to principles that can be universally applied. Kantian justice focuses on the inherent worth of individuals and the necessity of treating others as ends in themselves, not merely as means to an end.

John Rawls (1921 – 2002)

John Rawls revitalized discussions of justice in the 20th century with his seminal work "A Theory of Justice." Rawls introduces the concept of "justice as fairness," which he illustrates through the hypothetical "original position" and the "veil of ignorance." In this thought experiment, individuals choose principles of justice without knowing their own position in society, ensuring impartiality and fairness. Rawls argues for two principles of justice: equal basic liberties for all and the arrangement of social and economic inequalities to benefit the least advantaged members of society. His theory seeks to balance liberty and equality, aiming to create a just society through fair distribution and respect for individual rights.

Crazy Facts About Justice

1. **Trial by Ordeal**: In medieval Europe, "trial by ordeal" was a method used to determine guilt or innocence. Accused individuals underwent dangerous or painful tests, such as carrying a hot iron or being submerged in water, with the belief that divine intervention would reveal the truth.
2. **Draco's Laws**: Ancient Athenian lawmaker Draco implemented a legal code in 621 BCE known for its harshness. The term "draconian" comes from Draco's laws, which were so severe that even minor offenses were punishable by death.
3. **The Great Law of Peace**: The Iroquois Confederacy's constitution, known as the Great Law of Peace, influenced the development of democratic principles in the United States. This Native American legal system emphasized equality, justice, and the welfare of the community.
4. **Solomon's Wisdom**: The biblical story of King Solomon's judgment showcases an early example of wisdom in justice. When two women claimed to be the mother of a baby, Solomon suggested dividing the child in two. The true mother revealed herself by her willingness to give up her claim to save the child's life.
5. **Beccaria's Reforms**: Cesare Beccaria, an 18th-century Italian philosopher, authored "On Crimes and Punishments," advocating for criminal justice reform. His ideas influenced the abolition of torture and capital punishment in many countries, emphasizing the importance of proportionate punishment and the presumption of innocence.

33. Priming in Marketing: Enhancing Consumer Responses

Have you ever played the game where one person says a word, and the other immediately responds with the first thing that comes to mind? This simple exercise captures the essence of priming. In psychological terms, priming involves exposure to one stimulus influencing the response to another stimulus. This effect occurs because the initial stimulus activates related concepts in the brain, making them more accessible and influencing subsequent reactions. In the context of marketing, priming can be a powerful tool to subtly influence consumer behavior and decision-making.

The Science Behind Priming

Priming works by creating associations in the consumer's mind. When consumers are exposed to specific words, images, or sounds, it activates related concepts stored in their memory. For example, if a consumer sees the word "cozy" in an advertisement, it might prime them to think of warmth, comfort, and relaxation. This associative process can influence their perceptions and behaviors, making them more receptive to products or messages that align with these concepts. Psychology Today provides a clear illustration of this phenomenon: if two groups of people read the word "yellow" followed by either "sky" or "banana," the "yellow-banana" group will recognize "banana" faster because of the strong semantic association between the fruit and its color.

Marketers use various priming techniques to enhance the effectiveness of their campaigns. Visual priming involves using specific images or colors that evoke certain emotions or associations. For instance, a luxury brand might use the color gold in its advertisements to prime consumers to think of wealth and exclusivity. Verbal priming, on the other hand, uses carefully chosen words and phrases to create desired associations. A car company, for example, might use words like "freedom," "adventure," and "power" in its ads to prime consumers to associate their vehicles with those qualities. Environmental priming involves setting up the physical environment in a way that influences consumer behavior, such as using specific scents in stores to create a pleasant shopping experience.

Many world-famous businesses have successfully leveraged priming in their marketing strategies. One notable example is **Coca-Cola**. The company uses the color red extensively in its branding, which is known to stimulate excitement and energy, priming consumers to associate the drink with these feelings. Another example is **Apple**, which uses sleek, minimalist designs and the color white in its marketing materials to prime consumers to think of innovation, simplicity, and high quality. **McDonald's** also effectively uses priming by incorporating the color yellow and the golden arches in its branding, which are associated with happiness and positivity, priming consumers to feel good about their dining experience.

The impact of priming on consumer behavior can be profound. When done effectively, priming can increase brand recognition, enhance product appeal, and drive purchase decisions. For instance, a study might show that consumers primed with words related to cleanliness are more likely to buy cleaning products. By understanding and utilizing priming techniques, marketers can create more effective campaigns that tap into consumers' subconscious associations, leading to more favorable responses and increased sales.

1. Coca-Cola:

Uses the color red to stimulate excitement and energy, creating a strong association with happiness and celebration.

2. Apple:

Employs sleek, minimalist designs and the color white to prime consumers to think of innovation, simplicity, and premium quality.

3. McDonald's:

Incorporates the color yellow and golden arches to evoke feelings of happiness and positivity, enhancing the overall dining experience.

4. Nike:

Uses motivational slogans and high-energy imagery in its advertisements to prime consumers to associate their products with athleticism, determination, and success.

5. Starbucks:

Employs earthy tones and comfortable, inviting store environments to prime consumers to associate their coffee experience with relaxation and indulgence.

6. Disney:

Uses enchanting music and magical imagery in its marketing to prime consumers to associate their brand with wonder, joy, and childhood dreams.

7. BMW:

Employs sleek, powerful car imagery and the color black to prime consumers to think of luxury, performance, and status.

8. Amazon:

Uses convenient, one-click purchasing options and the color orange to prime consumers to associate the brand with ease of use, speed, and reliability.

9. Whole Foods:

Incorporates natural colors and earthy designs in their stores and marketing materials to prime consumers to associate the brand with health, freshness, and sustainability.

10. IKEA:

Uses homey, relatable room setups and the color blue to prime consumers to think of comfort, practicality, and affordability in home furnishing.

Did You Know?

- Colors Have a Huge Impact: Did you know that color can influence consumer behavior? Studies have shown that up to 90% of snap judgments made about products can be based on color alone. For example, the color red can create a sense of urgency, which is why it's often used in clearance sales.
- The Power of Placement: Products placed at eye level are more likely to be purchased. This is why brands often pay premium prices for shelf space that is directly in the line of sight of shoppers, maximizing visibility and sales.
- Decoy Pricing: Some businesses use decoy pricing to steer customers towards a more profitable option. By presenting three pricing options, with the middle one offering more value for just a bit more money than the lowest option, consumers often choose the middle one, thinking they are getting a better deal.
- Endowment Effect: When people own something, they value it more highly. This is why free trials or money-back guarantees are effective. Once customers start using a product, they are more likely to want to keep it, feeling a greater sense of ownership.
- The Rule of 7: Research suggests that a potential customer needs to see or hear your marketing message at least seven times before they take action. This is known as the Rule of 7 in marketing, emphasizing the importance of repeated exposure.

34. The Philosophy of Language

The philosophy of language explores the nature, origins, and use of language, delving into how words and sentences convey meaning. This branch of philosophy intersects with linguistics, cognitive science, and logic, examining fundamental questions about the relationship between language, thought, and reality. Philosophers in this field investigate how language structures our understanding of the world and how linguistic expressions correlate with mental and social phenomena.

One of the seminal figures in the philosophy of language is Ludwig Wittgenstein. His early work, "Tractatus Logico-Philosophicus," posits that language mirrors reality through logical structures. Wittgenstein later revised his views in "Philosophical Investigations," where he argued that the meaning of words is rooted in their use within specific social practices, coining the term "language games." This shift highlights the pragmatic aspect of language, suggesting that meaning is not an inherent property of words but is shaped by their function in various forms of life.

Another critical figure is Ferdinand de Saussure, whose work laid the foundation for structural linguistics. Saussure introduced the concept of the linguistic sign, which comprises the "signifier" (the form of a word) and the "signified" (the concept it represents). He emphasized that the relationship between signifier and signified is arbitrary, meaning that words have no intrinsic connection to their referents. This insight underscores the role of social conventions in language and the dynamic nature of linguistic systems.

In contemporary philosophy, Noam Chomsky's theories have had a profound impact. Chomsky introduced the idea of an innate "universal grammar," suggesting that the ability to acquire language is hardwired into the human brain. According to Chomsky, all human languages share a common structural basis, reflecting an underlying cognitive framework. This perspective has influenced debates on the nature of linguistic competence and the interplay between language and thought.

The philosophy of language also engages with issues of meaning, reference, and truth. Philosophers like Saul Kripke and Hilary Putnam have challenged traditional views with their theories of reference, arguing that names and natural kind terms directly refer to objects and kinds in the world without needing descriptive content. This direct reference theory has implications for understanding how language relates to the external world and how truth conditions for statements are determined.

- **Wittgenstein's Transformation**: Ludwig Wittgenstein underwent a significant shift in his thinking about language. His early work suggested a strict logical structure, while his later work focused on the practical use of language in everyday life, showing the evolution of his philosophical views.
- **The Sapir-Whorf Hypothesis**: This hypothesis, developed by Edward Sapir and Benjamin Lee Whorf, suggests that the structure of a language affects its speakers' worldview and cognition. It proposes that language shapes thought, influencing how people perceive and categorize the world.
- **Chomsky's Universal Grammar**: Noam Chomsky's theory of universal grammar posits that the ability to learn language is innate to humans and that all languages share a common structural basis. This idea revolutionized the study of linguistics and cognitive science.
- **Speech Act Theory**: Proposed by philosophers like J.L. Austin and John Searle, speech act theory examines how utterances perform actions. For example, saying "I promise" is not just stating a fact but actually performing the act of promising, highlighting the performative nature of language.

35. Who Was Confucius?

Confucius (551-479 BCE) was a Chinese philosopher, teacher, and political figure whose thoughts have deeply influenced Chinese culture and beyond. Born in the small state of Lu, now part of modern-day Shandong Province, Confucius lived during a time of significant social and political upheaval known as the Spring and Autumn period. Despite the chaotic context of his life, his ideas centered on morality, social relationships, and justice, seeking to restore order and harmony in society.

Confucius was born into a relatively humble family, but his father, a warrior, died when Confucius was young. Despite financial hardships, Confucius was dedicated to learning and self-improvement from an early age. His mother's influence played a crucial role in his early education, instilling in him the values of hard work and perseverance. As a young man, Confucius worked in various government roles, including as a manager of state granaries and livestock, and eventually rose to higher administrative positions.

Confucius's teachings, known as Confucianism, focus on personal and governmental morality, the correctness of social relationships, justice, and sincerity. His philosophy is built upon the idea of **Ren** (仁), often translated as "benevolence" or "humaneness," which emphasizes compassion and empathy towards others. Another key concept is **Li** (礼), meaning "ritual" or "propriety," which refers to the proper conduct in social and ceremonial contexts. Confucius believed that adherence to these principles would lead to a harmonious society.

The Five Relationships

Central to Confucian thought is the importance of relationships and the roles individuals play within them. Confucius outlined five key relationships that he believed were the foundation of a stable society:

1. **Ruler and subject**
2. **Father and son**
3. **Husband and wife**
4. **Older brother and younger brother**
5. **Friend and friend**

Each relationship is characterized by a set of duties and responsibilities, emphasizing mutual respect and proper conduct.

Although Confucius did not gain significant recognition during his lifetime, his teachings were collected and preserved by his disciples in texts such as the **Analects** (Lunyu). Over the centuries, Confucianism became the dominant philosophical system in China, deeply influencing Chinese education, governance, and social structure. The Confucian examination system became a key part of the Chinese civil service, shaping the intellectual and political landscape for millennia.

Confucianism has had a profound impact not only in China but also in other East Asian countries, including Korea, Japan, and Vietnam. Its emphasis on education, family loyalty, and ethical governance has permeated various aspects of culture and society in these regions. In modern times, Confucian ideals continue to be relevant, contributing to discussions on morality, ethics, and the role of education in personal and social development.

1. **Confucian Examination System**: The civil service examination system in China, heavily influenced by Confucian thought, lasted for over 1,300 years and was used to select government officials based on merit rather than birthright.
2. **Confucius Institutes**: There are now hundreds of Confucius Institutes around the world, promoting Chinese language and culture, reflecting the global influence of Confucian philosophy.
3. **Confucius's Disciples**: Confucius had many disciples who helped spread his teachings. The most famous among them were the Four Sages: Yan Hui, Zengzi, Zisi, and Mencius, who further developed and interpreted Confucian thought.

4. **Temple of Confucius**: The Temple of Confucius in Qufu, his birthplace, is one of the largest and most significant Confucian temples. It is a UNESCO World Heritage Site and a testament to his enduring legacy.

Confucius's teachings continue to inspire and guide individuals and societies, emphasizing the importance of moral integrity, education, and respectful relationships. His vision of a harmonious society built on ethical principles remains a cornerstone of East Asian culture and thought.

> "Is it not a pleasure, having learned something, to try it out at due intervals? Is it not a joy to have friends come from afar? Is it not gentlemanly not to take offense when others fail to appreciate your abilities?"
>
> **- Confucius**

This quote reflects Confucius's belief in continuous learning, the value of friendship, and the importance of humility and understanding in social interactions. It underscores his emphasis on personal improvement, harmonious relationships, and ethical conduct as essential components of a virtuous life.

36. The Fascination with True Crime Stories

True crime stories have long captivated audiences, weaving together the elements of mystery, human psychology, and societal intrigue. From books and documentaries to podcasts and television series, the genre of true crime has become a significant cultural phenomenon. But what drives our collective fascination with these often dark and disturbing tales?

One of the primary reasons people are drawn to true crime stories is the allure of mystery. True crime narratives often present a puzzle that needs solving, engaging the audience's curiosity and problem-solving skills. The process of uncovering clues, piecing together evidence, and ultimately discovering the truth behind a crime provides a mental challenge that many find irresistibly engaging. This sense of mystery not only keeps the audience on the edge of their seats but also stimulates cognitive engagement and critical thinking.

True crime stories offer a deep dive into the human psyche, providing insight into the minds of both perpetrators and victims. Understanding the motivations behind criminal behavior, the psychological profiles of offenders, and the impact of crime on victims and their families offers a compelling exploration of human nature. This psychological dimension appeals to our innate curiosity about what drives people to commit such acts and how different individuals respond to extreme situations. It also allows for a vicarious experience of fear and danger within the safe confines of storytelling.

Engaging with true crime often leads to reflection on moral and ethical issues. These stories force us to confront uncomfortable questions about justice, morality, and human nature. They challenge our perceptions of good and evil, right and wrong, and the complexities that lie in between. By examining real-life cases, audiences can reflect on the adequacy of the legal system, the nature of punishment and redemption, and the societal factors that contribute to criminal behavior. This ethical reflection can be both thought-provoking and educational, fostering a deeper understanding of the social constructs around crime and justice.

True crime stories also elicit strong emotional responses, including empathy and identification. Hearing the personal stories of victims, their struggles, and the impact of the crimes on their lives and communities creates a profound emotional connection. This empathy can lead to a greater awareness and understanding of the experiences of others, promoting social empathy and compassion. For some, these stories also serve as a way to process their own fears and anxieties, finding solace in the resolution of these narratives.

The fascination with true crime extends beyond individual interest, fostering a sense of community among enthusiasts. Online forums, social media groups, and fan conventions provide platforms for people to discuss theories, share new cases, and connect with like-minded individuals. This communal aspect adds a layer of social interaction and shared experience, enhancing the appeal of true crime. The genre also reflects and shapes cultural attitudes towards crime and justice, influencing public perception and sometimes even policy.

- **Origins of the Genre**: The true crime genre dates back centuries. One of the earliest examples is "The Newgate Calendar," a popular 18th-century publication that detailed the lives and crimes of notorious criminals in England.
- **The Role of Podcasts**: The rise of podcasts has significantly boosted the popularity of true crime. Shows like "Serial," which re-examined a cold murder case, have reached millions of listeners and sparked renewed interest in the genre.
- **Impact on Legal Cases**: True crime media has influenced real-life legal proceedings. Documentaries such as "Making a Murderer" and "The Jinx" have led to new evidence

coming to light and even resulted in retrials and changes in legal outcomes.
- **Psychological Effects**: Consuming true crime content can have psychological effects, both positive and negative. While it can heighten awareness and safety precautions, excessive consumption may also lead to increased anxiety and fearfulness about crime.

While the fascination with true crime can be enlightening and entertaining, there are instances where it has crossed ethical boundaries and exploited sensitive subjects. One notable example is the case of the Netflix documentary series "Don't F**k with Cats: Hunting an Internet Killer," which sparked controversy and raised ethical concerns due to its graphic content and the sensationalization of a disturbing murder case.

In this series, viewers were taken on a journey where online communities tracked down a man responsible for heinous acts of animal cruelty and later a murder. While the intention was to explore the power of online communities in solving crimes, the graphic depiction of animal abuse and the focus on the perpetrator's motivations crossed into exploitative territory. Critics argued that the series not only glorified the killer by giving him extensive screen time but also potentially encouraged copycat behavior by showcasing the infamy that can come from committing such atrocities.

Another instance where the true crime genre went too far involves cases where victims' families were not properly consulted or their wishes disregarded in the pursuit of sensational storytelling. The media's relentless focus on the personal tragedies of victims without their families' consent can lead to re-traumatization and ethical dilemmas. Sensationalized narratives that prioritize shocking details over respect for the victims' dignity and privacy can undermine the very real human suffering involved in these cases.

37. Sigmund Freud Through Quotes

Sigmund Freud (1856-1939) was an Austrian neurologist who is widely regarded as the father of psychoanalysis. His theories on the unconscious mind, defense mechanisms, and the significance of dreams revolutionized the understanding of human psychology. Freud's work has had a profound impact on both psychology and Western thought. Here, we explore his life and ideas through some of his most famous quotes, shedding light on his contributions to the field.

> *"The mind is like an iceberg, it floats with one-seventh of its bulk above water."*

This quote illustrates Freud's belief that the conscious mind is only a small part of our mental activity, with the vast majority lying beneath the surface in the unconscious. He argued that unconscious thoughts and desires significantly influence behavior and personality.

> *"Unexpressed emotions will never die. They are buried alive and will come forth later in uglier ways."*

Freud emphasized the importance of acknowledging and addressing repressed emotions. He believed that unacknowledged feelings could manifest later in life as psychological disturbances or neurotic behavior, highlighting the need for therapeutic intervention.

"Dreams are the royal road to the unconscious."

Freud viewed dreams as a window into the unconscious mind, revealing hidden desires and thoughts. His work "The Interpretation of Dreams" laid the foundation for understanding how dreams reflect our deepest wishes and fears, often disguised in symbolic form.

"In the small matters trust the mind, in the large ones the heart."

This quote underscores Freud's belief in the significance of the unconscious mind, particularly in making crucial life decisions. He suggested that our deepest, often unarticulated, feelings play a critical role in guiding our actions and choices.

"Where id was, there ego shall be."

Freud's famous dictum encapsulates the goal of psychoanalysis: to bring unconscious desires (the id) into the realm of the conscious mind (the ego), allowing individuals to understand and manage their inner conflicts. This process aims to achieve greater self-awareness and psychological health.

"One day, in retrospect, the years of struggle will strike you as the most beautiful."

Freud acknowledged the challenging nature of psychoanalysis and personal growth. He believed that facing and overcoming internal struggles could lead to profound personal development and a deeper appreciation of life's journey.

> *"The first human who hurled an insult instead of a stone was the founder of civilization."*

Freud often explored the interplay between individual instincts and societal norms. This quote reflects his view that the sublimation of aggressive impulses into socially acceptable behavior is a cornerstone of human civilization.

> *"Most people do not really want freedom, because freedom involves responsibility, and most people are frightened of responsibility."*

Freud's insights into human nature often revealed uncomfortable truths about the human psyche. He believed that many individuals resist true freedom due to the inherent responsibilities and potential anxieties it entails.

> *"Civilization began the first time an angry person cast a word instead of a rock."*

Freud saw the development of communication and the management of primal instincts as fundamental to the progress of civilization. His work often highlighted the tension between our basic drives and the demands of social order.

Freud's ideas have sparked both admiration and controversy, shaping the course of modern psychology and influencing various disciplines, including literature, art, and cultural studies. His exploration of the unconscious, the significance of dreams, and the complexities of human behavior continue to be foundational in psychoanalytic theory and therapy.

- **Freud's Major Works**: Some of Freud's most influential works include "The Interpretation of Dreams" (1900), "The Psychopathology of Everyday Life" (1901), and "Beyond the Pleasure Principle" (1920). These texts have been critical in developing the field of psychoanalysis and understanding human psychology.
- **Defense Mechanisms**: Freud introduced the concept of defense mechanisms, unconscious strategies used by the ego to protect itself from anxiety. These include repression, denial, projection, and sublimation, which are still widely referenced in psychological literature today.
- **Freudian Slip**: The term "Freudian slip" originates from Freud's theory that errors in speech or memory reveal unconscious thoughts or desires. These slips are seen as windows into the hidden workings of the mind.
- **Controversial Theories**: Some of Freud's theories, such as the Oedipus complex and his views on sexuality, have been widely debated and critiqued. Despite this, his contributions to understanding the human mind and behavior remain invaluable and influential.

38. The Stanford Prison Experiment: A Fascinating Study in Psychology

One of the most fascinating and controversial studies in the field of psychology is the Stanford Prison Experiment, conducted by psychologist Philip Zimbardo in 1971. This study aimed to explore the psychological effects of perceived power, focusing on the struggle between prisoners and prison guards. It provides profound insights into how situational factors can influence human behavior, often leading to unexpected and alarming outcomes.

The Setup

The experiment took place in the basement of the psychology department at Stanford University, which was converted into a mock prison. Zimbardo and his team selected 24 male college students who were deemed psychologically stable and healthy. These participants were randomly assigned to either the role of prisoner or guard to simulate a real-life prison environment.

The guards were given uniforms, whistles, and reflective sunglasses to prevent eye contact, symbolizing their authority. The prisoners were dressed in smocks with identification numbers, creating a sense of dehumanization. The guards were instructed to maintain order without using physical violence, while the prisoners were subjected to the rules and regulations of the prison environment.

The Course of the Experiment

The experiment was initially planned to last for two weeks, but it was terminated after only six days due to the extreme and distressing behaviors exhibited by the participants. Within a short period, the guards began to adopt authoritarian and abusive behaviors, while the prisoners showed signs of severe emotional distress and helplessness.

- **Day 1-2**: The prisoners began to rebel against the guards' authority, resulting in the guards employing psychological tactics to maintain control, such as creating privileges for compliant prisoners and punishments for disobedient ones.
- **Day 3-4**: The guards' behavior became increasingly sadistic. They forced prisoners to perform degrading tasks, imposed solitary confinement, and restricted bathroom access. The prisoners, in turn, became more passive and despondent.
- **Day 5-6**: The emotional breakdowns among prisoners became more frequent. Several participants had to be released early due to extreme emotional reactions, including crying, rage, and acute anxiety. Realizing the experiment's harmful impact, Zimbardo decided to end it prematurely.

Key Findings and Implications

The Stanford Prison Experiment demonstrated the powerful influence of situational factors and social roles on human behavior. The following key findings emerged:

- **Deindividuation**: The guards' uniforms and the prisoners' numbered smocks contributed to a loss of personal identity, leading to behaviors inconsistent with participants' usual personalities. This process, known as deindividuation, can reduce self-awareness and lead to a diminished sense of personal responsibility.
- **Conformity to Roles**: Both guards and prisoners conformed to their assigned roles with alarming ease, highlighting the

impact of social expectations and group dynamics on individual actions. The experiment showed how people could quickly adopt behaviors that align with their perceived roles, even if these behaviors contradict their moral beliefs.
- **Power Dynamics**: The study illustrated how power dynamics could corrupt individuals, with the guards displaying increasingly abusive behavior despite the absence of pre-existing tendencies toward such actions. It underscored the potential for systemic abuse in environments where authority is unchecked.
- **Ethical Concerns**: The experiment raised significant ethical questions regarding the treatment of participants in psychological research. The extreme stress and emotional trauma experienced by participants highlighted the need for stringent ethical standards and oversight in research involving human subjects.

Statistics and Follow-Up Studies

- **Participant Breakdown**: Of the 24 participants, 9 guards and 9 prisoners were involved in the daily operations, with the remaining participants on standby. Over the course of the experiment, several prisoners were released early due to severe emotional distress.
- **Behavioral Changes**: According to post-experiment interviews, many guards reported being surprised by their own aggressive behavior, while prisoners expressed shock at their submissiveness and emotional breakdowns.
- **Long-Term Impact**: Follow-up studies and interviews with participants revealed lasting effects on their perceptions of authority and power. The experiment continues to be a point of reference in discussions about the influence of situational factors on behavior.

Controversy and Criticism

Despite its profound insights, the Stanford Prison Experiment has faced considerable criticism:

- **Methodological Flaws**: Critics argue that the experiment's design, including the lack of clear guidelines and the role of Zimbardo as both researcher and prison superintendent, may have influenced participants' behavior.
- **Ethical Violations**: The extreme psychological stress inflicted on participants has been widely condemned, leading to calls for more rigorous ethical standards in psychological research.
- **Replicability Issues**: Attempts to replicate the experiment have yielded mixed results, raising questions about the generalizability of its findings.

The Stanford Prison Experiment remains one of the most compelling and controversial studies in psychology. Its exploration of the impact of situational factors on behavior has provided valuable insights into human nature, power dynamics, and the ethical considerations of psychological research. Despite its flaws, the experiment continues to serve as a critical reference point in understanding the complex interplay between individual dispositions and social environments.

39. The Milgram Experiment: A Landmark Study in Psychology

Another landmark study in psychology that has generated significant interest and debate is the Milgram Experiment, conducted by psychologist Stanley Milgram in the early 1960s. This study aimed to investigate the extent to which individuals would obey authority figures, even when instructed to perform actions conflicting with their personal conscience. The findings of the Milgram Experiment have had profound implications for understanding authority, obedience, and ethical behavior.

The Setup

The Milgram Experiment was conducted at Yale University, where participants were recruited through newspaper ads and mail solicitations, offering payment for their participation. The study involved three roles: the experimenter (an authority figure in a lab coat), the teacher (the real participant), and the learner (an actor pretending to be a participant). The participants were told that the study aimed to examine the effects of punishment on learning.

The teacher was instructed to administer electric shocks to the learner for every incorrect answer in a word-pairing task. The shocks were to increase in intensity with each mistake, starting from 15 volts and going up to a maximum of 450 volts. Unbeknownst to the teacher, the learner was not actually receiving any shocks but was instead acting out responses to the supposed shocks, including expressions of pain and distress.

The Course of the Experiment

Participants were placed in front of a shock generator with switches labeled with voltage levels, ranging from slight shock to severe shock, and even a danger warning for the highest levels. As the learner (actor) purposely gave incorrect answers, the experimenter would instruct the teacher to deliver increasingly higher shocks.

- **Initial Compliance**: At the lower shock levels, most participants complied without hesitation. The learner would start to show signs of discomfort, which was acted out convincingly.
- **Escalation**: As the voltage increased, the learner's responses became more dramatic, including pounding on the wall and pleading to stop the experiment. Despite this, many participants continued to administer shocks when urged by the experimenter.
- **Critical Points**: When the shocks reached higher levels, many participants expressed concern or questioned the procedure. However, when the experimenter insisted with phrases such as "The experiment requires that you continue," or "You have no other choice, you must go on," a significant number of participants continued to obey.

Key Findings and Implications

The Milgram Experiment revealed startling insights into human behavior, demonstrating that ordinary people could perform acts that conflicted with their morals when instructed by an authority figure. The key findings include:

- **High Rates of Obedience**: Approximately 65% of participants continued to the highest shock level of 450 volts, despite hearing the learner's screams and pleas. All participants administered shocks up to 300 volts.

- **Role of Authority**: The experiment underscored the powerful influence of authority figures on individual behavior. Participants often deferred to the experimenter's commands, even when they felt uncomfortable or morally conflicted.
- **Ethical and Psychological Impact**: Many participants experienced significant stress and emotional conflict during the experiment. Milgram's findings raised important ethical questions about the treatment of human subjects in psychological research.

Statistics and Follow-Up Studies

- **Participant Breakdown**: A total of 40 male participants were involved in the original study. Subsequent variations included different demographics and settings to test the consistency of the findings.
- **Behavioral Observations**: Post-experiment interviews revealed that many participants were distressed by their actions, yet felt compelled to follow the experimenter's instructions due to the perceived authority.
- **Repetition and Variation**: Follow-up studies and replications of the Milgram Experiment in different cultures and contexts generally confirmed the original findings, highlighting the universal aspects of obedience to authority.

Controversy and Criticism

Despite its influential findings, the Milgram Experiment has faced considerable criticism:

- **Ethical Concerns**: The study's methods, particularly the deception involved and the emotional stress inflicted on participants, have been widely condemned. This has led to stricter ethical guidelines for psychological research.

- **Methodological Issues**: Critics argue that the artificial setting of the experiment may not accurately reflect real-world scenarios. Additionally, the level of authority and coercion exerted by the experimenter has been questioned.
- **Generalizability**: While follow-up studies have largely supported Milgram's findings, some variations have shown lower levels of obedience, suggesting that context and individual differences can significantly impact behavior.

The Milgram Experiment remains a seminal study in psychology, offering profound insights into the nature of authority and obedience. It highlights the capacity for ordinary individuals to commit acts they might otherwise consider immoral when directed by an authority figure. Despite ethical concerns and methodological critiques, the study continues to be a critical reference point in discussions about human behavior, ethics, and the power of authority. Its implications extend to various fields, including social psychology, ethics, and organizational behavior.

"The social psychology of this century reveals a major lesson: often it is not so much the kind of person a man is as the kind of situation in which he finds himself that determines how he will act."

- Stanley Milgram

This quote encapsulates one of the central findings of the Milgram Experiment, emphasizing the profound influence of situational factors, such as authority, on individual behavior. It underscores Milgram's belief that human actions can be deeply influenced by the social context in which they occur, even overriding personal moral considerations.

40. The Science of Decision Fatigue

Decision fatigue refers to the deteriorating quality of decisions made by an individual after a long session of decision-making. It is a psychological phenomenon where the more decisions we make, the more our ability to make further decisions becomes compromised. This effect can lead to poorer decision-making and impulsive choices, impacting both our personal and professional lives.

Understanding Decision Fatigue

The concept of decision fatigue is rooted in the idea that human beings have a limited amount of mental energy for making decisions. Each decision, whether minor or significant, depletes a bit of this cognitive resource. As the day progresses and decisions accumulate, our mental energy diminishes, leading to an increased likelihood of making hasty, poorly thought-out choices. This depletion can result in reduced self-control, impacting areas such as diet, spending habits, and productivity.

Psychological Mechanisms

One of the key mechanisms behind decision fatigue is the depletion of glucose in the brain. Studies have shown that the act of making decisions consumes glucose, the brain's primary energy source. As glucose levels drop, cognitive functions, including decision-making, become impaired. This is why after a long day of making numerous decisions, people may feel mentally exhausted and resort to easier, less optimal choices.

Another mechanism is ego depletion, a concept suggesting that self-control and decision-making draw upon a shared pool of cognitive resources. When these resources are drained through prolonged decision-making or exerting self-control, our ability to continue making sound decisions diminishes. This can lead to impulsive behaviors and a reliance on default or habitual responses.

Impact on Daily Life

Decision fatigue can manifest in various aspects of daily life. In professional settings, it can affect productivity and decision quality, leading to errors and suboptimal choices. For instance, judges have been found to make more favorable rulings earlier in the day, with decisions becoming harsher as fatigue sets in. In personal life, decision fatigue can influence dietary choices, leading individuals to opt for unhealthy foods that require less mental effort to decide upon.

Marketers often exploit decision fatigue by timing their advertisements and sales pitches when consumers are more likely to be mentally exhausted. This increases the chances of impulsive purchases, as tired consumers are less able to resist temptation. Understanding the dynamics of decision fatigue can help individuals and organizations develop strategies to mitigate its effects, such as prioritizing important decisions earlier in the day and simplifying choices.

1. **Parole Decisions**: A study found that judges were more likely to grant parole earlier in the day, with approval rates dropping significantly as the day progressed. This highlights how decision fatigue can impact even critical, high-stakes decisions.
2. **Consumer Behavior**: Supermarkets often place impulse-buy items like candy and snacks near the checkout area to capitalize on decision fatigue. After making numerous choices while shopping, consumers are more likely to make impulsive purchases at the end of their trip.

3. **Workplace Efficiency**: Decision fatigue can be mitigated in the workplace by reducing the number of decisions employees need to make. Implementing routines and automating tasks can help conserve cognitive resources for more important decisions.
4. **Presidential Habits**: Former President Barack Obama famously reduced decision fatigue by limiting his wardrobe choices, often wearing only gray or blue suits. By minimizing trivial decisions, he could conserve mental energy for more significant matters.

Decision fatigue is a significant factor in our cognitive and behavioral patterns, influencing a wide range of activities and decisions. By recognizing its effects and implementing strategies to manage decision-making processes, we can improve our overall decision quality and maintain better control over our choices.

Did you know

That decision fatigue can influence our judicial system in surprising ways? Research has shown that parole boards are more likely to grant parole earlier in the day or after breaks, when decision-makers are less fatigued. As the day progresses and decision fatigue sets in, the likelihood of favorable rulings decreases significantly. This phenomenon underscores how even critical decisions regarding someone's freedom can be unintentionally influenced by the mental exhaustion caused by decision fatigue.

41. The Idea of Utopia and Dystopia

The concepts of utopia and dystopia have long fascinated philosophers, writers, and thinkers. Utopia represents an ideal society, a perfect world where everything functions harmoniously for the benefit of all its inhabitants. In contrast, dystopia portrays a nightmarish society, characterized by oppression, injustice, and widespread suffering. Different philosophers and thinkers have explored these concepts, offering diverse perspectives on what constitutes an ideal or flawed society.

Plato (428/427 – 348/347 BCE)

Utopia: The Republic

Plato's "The Republic" is one of the earliest works to describe a utopian society. In this dialogue, Plato outlines his vision of an ideal state ruled by philosopher-kings. He proposes a rigid class structure with a ruling class of philosopher-guardians, a warrior class, and a producing class. The society is governed by reason and justice, with communal ownership and the abolition of private property to eliminate inequality and conflict. Education and the nurturing of the soul are paramount, ensuring that each individual fulfills their role for the greater good.

Key Ideas:

- **Philosopher-Kings**: Wise and just rulers guided by reason.
- **Class Structure**: Each class performing its designated role harmoniously.

- **Communal Living**: Elimination of private property to prevent greed and discord.

Thomas More (1478 – 1535)

Utopia: Utopia

Thomas More's "Utopia," published in 1516, presents a detailed description of an imaginary island society that embodies his vision of an ideal community. More's utopia features religious tolerance, communal ownership, and a welfare state that ensures everyone's needs are met. The citizens live simple, virtuous lives, working only six hours a day and spending the rest of their time in intellectual pursuits. There is no private property, and goods are stored in warehouses where people take what they need.

Key Ideas:

- **Communal Ownership**: No private property, communal distribution of goods.
- **Work-Life Balance**: Short working hours and emphasis on intellectual activities.
- **Religious Tolerance**: Acceptance of various religious beliefs.

Karl Marx (1818 – 1883)

Utopia: Classless Society

Karl Marx envisioned a utopian society as a classless, stateless community where the means of production are communally owned. In works like "The Communist Manifesto" and "Das Kapital," Marx outlines his belief that the abolition of private property and the overthrow of capitalist systems would lead to a society where resources are distributed according to need. In this ideal communist society, there would be no class struggles, and people would work in harmony for the collective good.

Key Ideas:

- **Classless Society**: Elimination of class distinctions.
- **Communal Ownership**: Means of production owned collectively.
- **Distribution According to Need**: Resources allocated based on individual needs.

George Orwell (1903 – 1950)

Dystopia: 1984

George Orwell's "1984" presents a grim vision of a dystopian future where totalitarianism reigns supreme. The novel depicts a society controlled by a single-party dictatorship led by Big Brother. The government exercises absolute power through surveillance, propaganda, and the suppression of dissent. Individuality and independent thought are crushed, and language is manipulated to limit freedom of expression and thought. Orwell's work serves as a warning about the dangers of totalitarianism and the erosion of personal freedoms.

Key Ideas:

- **Totalitarian Control**: Government surveillance and oppression.
- **Manipulation of Truth**: Propaganda and control of information.
- **Suppression of Individuality**: Elimination of personal freedoms.

Aldous Huxley (1894 – 1963)

Dystopia: Brave New World

Aldous Huxley's "Brave New World" explores a dystopian society driven by technological advancements and state control. In this world, people are engineered through genetic manipulation and conditioned for their roles in society. The government maintains control through the use of a pleasure-inducing drug called soma, which keeps the populace docile and content. Individuality and emotional depth are sacrificed for stability and superficial happiness. Huxley's dystopia highlights the dangers of sacrificing humanity for technological progress and societal control.

Key Ideas:

- **Technological Control**: Genetic engineering and societal conditioning.
- **State-Induced Happiness**: Use of drugs to maintain social order.
- **Loss of Individuality**: Sacrifice of personal identity for societal stability.

Fyodor Dostoevsky (1821 – 1881)

Dystopia: Notes from Underground

In "Notes from Underground," Fyodor Dostoevsky presents a critical view of utopianism by exploring the psychological complexities of human nature. The protagonist, an unnamed narrator, rejects the idea of a perfect society, arguing that humans are inherently irrational and driven by a desire for free will, even if it leads to suffering. Dostoevsky's work questions the feasibility of utopian ideals and emphasizes the unpredictable and contradictory aspects of human behavior.

Key Ideas:

- **Rejection of Utopianism**: Skepticism about the possibility of a perfect society.
- **Human Irrationality**: Emphasis on the irrational and contradictory nature of humans.
- **Value of Free Will**: Importance of individual freedom, even with its inherent challenges.

The Term "Utopia": Coined by Thomas More, "utopia" is derived from the Greek words "ou" (not) and "topos" (place), meaning "no place" or "nowhere." It suggests that a perfect society is an unattainable ideal.

Dystopian Literature: Often reflects contemporary societal fears and critiques. For example, Orwell's "1984" was influenced by the rise of totalitarian regimes in the 20th century, while Huxley's "Brave New World" comments on consumerism and the loss of individuality.

Utopian Experiments: There have been real-life attempts to create utopian communities, such as the 19th-century Shaker villages in the United States and the Israeli kibbutzim, which sought to implement communal living and shared ownership.

Psychological Impact: Studies suggest that engaging with dystopian fiction can increase critical thinking and social awareness, as readers reflect on the societal issues depicted and draw parallels with their own world.

Exploring the ideas of utopia and dystopia through the lens of different philosophers provides a rich understanding of humanity's quest for an ideal society and the inherent challenges and dangers in such pursuits.

42. Do We Live in a Simulation? The Matrix Hypothesis

The idea that our reality might be a sophisticated computer simulation has intrigued philosophers, scientists, and popular culture alike. Known as the "Matrix Hypothesis," named after the 1999 film "The Matrix," this concept raises profound questions about the nature of existence, consciousness, and the limits of human knowledge. It challenges our perceptions and invites us to consider whether the world we experience is an elaborate illusion.

Philosophical Foundations

The roots of the simulation hypothesis can be traced back to ancient philosophy. Plato's Allegory of the Cave, presented in "The Republic," describes prisoners who perceive shadows on a cave wall as their reality, unaware of the true world outside. This allegory illustrates how our perceptions might be limited to mere reflections of a deeper, hidden reality. Similarly, René Descartes' famous dictum, "Cogito, ergo sum" (I think, therefore I am), emerged from his skepticism about the reliability of sensory experiences. Descartes imagined an evil demon capable of creating a complete illusion of the external world, prompting him to seek indubitable truths within his own consciousness.

Modern Simulation Hypothesis

In contemporary times, the simulation hypothesis was most notably articulated by philosopher Nick Bostrom in his 2003 paper "Are You Living in a Computer Simulation?" Bostrom proposes that at least one of the following propositions is true:

1. The human species is very likely to go extinct before reaching a "posthuman" stage.
2. Any posthuman civilization is extremely unlikely to run a significant number of simulations of their evolutionary history (or variations thereof).
3. We are almost certainly living in a computer simulation.

Bostrom argues that if future civilizations possess immense computational power and the inclination to run simulations of their ancestors, the number of simulated realities would vastly outnumber the single "base" reality. Consequently, it becomes statistically probable that we are living in one of these simulations.

Scientific and Technological Considerations

Advancements in technology lend some plausibility to the simulation hypothesis. The rapid progress in computer graphics, virtual reality, and artificial intelligence suggests that creating lifelike simulations of entire worlds could eventually become feasible. For example, contemporary video games and virtual reality environments already offer highly immersive experiences, and these technologies continue to improve.

Moreover, the concept of digital physics posits that the universe itself might operate on computational principles. Some physicists, such as John Archibald Wheeler with his "it from bit" theory, suggest that information is fundamental to the fabric of reality. This perspective aligns with the idea that our universe could be a digital construct.

Implications and Counterarguments

The simulation hypothesis raises numerous philosophical and ethical questions. If we are living in a simulation, what are the implications for concepts like free will, morality, and the search for meaning? Would it diminish the significance of human experiences, or would it simply shift our understanding of reality's nature?

Critics of the hypothesis argue that it is unfalsifiable and thus lacks empirical testability. Some contend that the hypothesis is a form of radical skepticism that leads to solipsism—the idea that only one's mind is sure to exist. Additionally, the sheer complexity and computational requirements of simulating an entire universe with conscious beings might be far beyond any conceivable future technology.

The simulation hypothesis has permeated popular culture, inspiring numerous works of fiction, including "The Matrix" trilogy, which vividly explores the concept of simulated reality.

- **Elon Musk's Belief**: Elon Musk, the CEO of SpaceX and Tesla, has publicly stated that he believes there is a high probability that we are living in a simulation. He argues that given the rapid advancement of technology, it's plausible that future civilizations could create highly realistic simulations.
- **Scientific Experiments**: Some physicists have proposed experiments to detect evidence of a simulated universe. For instance, researchers have suggested looking for anomalies in the distribution of cosmic rays, which might indicate underlying computational constraints.
- **Philosophical Debates**: The simulation hypothesis has sparked debates in philosophical circles about the nature of reality and epistemology. It challenges traditional notions of empirical evidence and raises questions about what can be known for certain.
- **Influence on AI Research**: The hypothesis has influenced discussions in artificial intelligence and consciousness studies. It raises intriguing possibilities about the nature of artificial entities and whether they could develop consciousness within simulated environments.

The Matrix Hypothesis remains a captivating and provocative idea, blending philosophy, science, and speculative fiction. Whether we live in a simulation or not, the exploration of this concept encourages deeper reflection on the nature of reality, the limits of human knowledge, and the potential future of technological advancements.

43. Who Was B. F. Skinner?

Burrhus Frederic Skinner (1904-1990), commonly known as B. F. Skinner, was an American psychologist, behaviorist, author, inventor, and social philosopher. He is best known for his work in behaviorism, a field of psychology that emphasizes the study of observable behaviors over internal mental processes. Skinner's contributions to psychology were groundbreaking, particularly his theories on operant conditioning, which have had a lasting impact on both psychology and education.

B. F. Skinner was born on March 20, 1904, in Susquehanna, Pennsylvania. He attended Hamilton College in New York, where he initially majored in English literature with the aim of becoming a writer. However, he soon became disillusioned with his literary aspirations. After earning his bachelor's degree in 1926, Skinner shifted his focus to psychology, inspired by the works of Ivan Pavlov and John B. Watson.

He pursued graduate studies at Harvard University, where he received his Ph.D. in psychology in 1931. At Harvard, Skinner conducted research under the supervision of renowned psychologist William Crozier, which laid the foundation for his later work in behaviorism.

Operant Conditioning

Skinner is most famous for developing the theory of operant conditioning, a method of learning that occurs through rewards and punishments for behavior. He proposed that behavior is a function of its consequences, and this relationship could be used to modify behavior through reinforcement and punishment. His work built on Edward Thorndike's law of effect, which states that behaviors followed by positive outcomes are likely to be repeated, while those followed by negative outcomes are less likely to be repeated.

To study operant conditioning, Skinner designed the "Skinner Box," a controlled environment where he could observe and measure animal behavior. The box typically contained a lever or button that an animal, such as a rat or pigeon, could press to receive a reward (food) or avoid a punishment (electric shock). Skinner demonstrated that animals could be trained to perform specific behaviors by manipulating the consequences of their actions.

Key Concepts in Skinner's Work

1. **Reinforcement**: Skinner identified two types of reinforcement—positive and negative. Positive reinforcement involves presenting a rewarding stimulus after a desired behavior, increasing the likelihood of that behavior being repeated. Negative reinforcement involves removing an aversive stimulus after a desired behavior, also increasing the likelihood of that behavior being repeated.
2. **Punishment**: Skinner also described two types of punishment—positive and negative. Positive punishment involves presenting an aversive stimulus after an undesired behavior, decreasing the likelihood of that behavior being repeated. Negative punishment involves removing a rewarding stimulus after an undesired behavior, also decreasing the likelihood of that behavior being repeated.
3. **Schedules of Reinforcement**: Skinner explored how different schedules of reinforcement affected learning and behavior. He found that continuous reinforcement (rewarding every correct response) led to faster learning, but behaviors were more resistant to extinction under partial reinforcement schedules (rewarding some, but not all, correct responses).

Skinner's work has had a profound impact on various fields, including psychology, education, and behavioral therapy. His principles of operant conditioning have been applied to classroom management, animal training, and the treatment of behavioral disorders. Skinner also extended his theories to human behavior, advocating for the use of behavior modification techniques to improve societal issues.

In addition to his work in psychology, Skinner was an advocate for social reform. He believed that behaviorism could be used to create a better society by designing environments that promoted positive behaviors and minimized negative ones. He explored these ideas in his utopian novel "Walden Two," which describes a community organized around behavioral principles.

1. **Air Crib**: Skinner invented the "air crib," also known as the "baby tender," a climate-controlled environment for infants designed to provide a safe and comfortable space. Despite some controversy, Skinner used it successfully with his own daughter.
2. **Pigeon Projects**: During World War II, Skinner worked on a project called "Project Pigeon," where he trained pigeons to guide missiles by pecking at a target on a screen. Although the project was never implemented, it demonstrated the potential for animal training in military applications.
3. **Behavioral Technology**: Skinner was a pioneer in the development of teaching machines and programmed instruction, which laid the groundwork for modern educational technology. His work emphasized the importance of immediate feedback and individualized learning.
4. **Criticism and Controversy**: Skinner's focus on observable behavior and dismissal of internal mental states garnered criticism from other psychologists who believed that cognition and emotions were crucial to understanding human behavior. Despite this, his contributions to behaviorism remain influential.

B. F. Skinner's theories and inventions have left an indelible mark on psychology, shaping our understanding of learning and behavior. His work continues to influence contemporary practices in education, therapy, and beyond, highlighting the enduring relevance of his contributions to the field.

44. Psychology Quiz

1. Which of the following is considered the father of psychoanalysis?

    a) Carl Jung
    b) Sigmund Freud
    c) Alfred Adler

2. What is the main focus of behaviorism in psychology?

    a) Inner mental processes
    b) Observable behaviors
    c) Childhood experiences

3. In Pavlov's experiments with dogs, what was the conditioned stimulus?

    a) Food
    b) Salivation
    c) Bell

4. Which neurotransmitter is primarily associated with mood regulation and is often targeted by antidepressants?

    a) Dopamine
    b) Serotonin
    c) Acetylcholine

5. The concept of "tabula rasa" or blank slate was proposed by which philosopher?

    a) John Locke
    b) Immanuel Kant
    c) René Descartes

6. Who developed the Hierarchy of Needs?

    a) B.F. Skinner
    b) Abraham Maslow

c) Carl Rogers

7. Which psychological disorder is characterized by periods of extreme highs and lows in mood?

   a) Schizophrenia
   b) Bipolar disorder
   c) Obsessive-compulsive disorder

8. In cognitive psychology, what does the term "schema" refer to?

   a) A sequence of events
   b) A mental framework for organizing information
   c) A stage of development

9. Who is known for the concept of the "collective unconscious"?

   a) Sigmund Freud
   b) Carl Jung
   c) Alfred Adler

10. The Stanford Prison Experiment was conducted by which psychologist?

   a) Stanley Milgram
   b) Philip Zimbardo
   c) John Watson

11. Which part of the brain is primarily responsible for forming new memories?

   a) Amygdala
   b) Hippocampus
   c) Thalamus

12. Which psychological perspective emphasizes the study of observable behavior and the effects of learning?

   a) Humanistic
   b) Psychodynamic
   c) Behaviorist

13. In developmental psychology, what is the term for the awareness that objects continue to exist even when they are not seen?

   a) Object permanence
   b) Conservation
   c) Assimilation

14. Which of the following describes a primary reinforcer?

   a) A stimulus that gains its reinforcing power through its association with a primary reinforcer
   b) A naturally reinforcing stimulus like food or water
   c) A stimulus presented after a response that increases the likelihood of that response recurring

15. Which of the following theories is most associated with Albert Bandura?

   a) Classical conditioning
   b) Operant conditioning
   c) Social learning theory

16. The "big five" personality traits do NOT include which of the following?

   a) Neuroticism
   b) Conscientiousness
   c) Introversion

17. Which branch of psychology focuses on the study of mental processes such as perception, memory, and reasoning?

   a) Cognitive psychology
   b) Behavioral psychology
   c) Developmental psychology

18. The term "functional fixedness" refers to:

a) The inability to see an object being used in a way other than its typical use
b) The tendency to only use objects in a familiar way
c) The tendency to solve problems using methods that have worked previously

19. What is the primary focus of industrial-organizational psychology?

a) Studying human behavior in the workplace
b) Understanding mental disorders
c) Exploring the human lifespan

20. Which famous psychologist is associated with the "Strange Situation" experiment?

a) Jean Piaget
b) Mary Ainsworth
c) Erik Erikson

Answers

1. b) Sigmund Freud
2. b) Observable behaviors
3. c) Bell
4. b) Serotonin
5. a) John Locke
6. b) Abraham Maslow
7. b) Bipolar disorder
8. b) A mental framework for organizing information
9. b) Carl Jung
10. b) Philip Zimbardo
11. b) Hippocampus
12. c) Behaviorist
13. a) Object permanence
14. b) A naturally reinforcing stimulus like food or water
15. c) Social learning theory
16. c) Introversion
17. a) Cognitive psychology
18. a) The inability to see an object being used in a way other than its typical use
19. a) Studying human behavior in the workplace
20. b) Mary Ainsworth

45. The Future of Philosophy

The future of philosophy will undoubtedly be shaped by rapid technological advancements. With the rise of artificial intelligence, biotechnology, and virtual reality, philosophers will be called upon to address the ethical implications of these innovations. Questions about AI consciousness, the moral status of genetically modified organisms, and the consequences of living in virtual worlds will challenge traditional philosophical paradigms. As technology blurs the lines between human and machine, philosophers will need to explore new frameworks for understanding identity, agency, and ethics.

Climate change and environmental degradation present urgent global challenges that philosophy must address. Environmental philosophy, which explores the ethical relationship between humans and the natural world, will gain increasing prominence. Philosophers will need to grapple with issues such as environmental justice, sustainability, and the moral obligations to future generations. As societies seek to balance economic development with ecological preservation, philosophical inquiry will be crucial in shaping policies and guiding ethical decision-making.

Globalization has interconnected the world in unprecedented ways, bringing diverse cultures into closer contact. This increased interaction will spur philosophical debates on multiculturalism, identity, and global ethics. Philosophers will need to engage with a broader range of perspectives, incorporating non-Western philosophies and addressing the complexities of cultural relativism. The future of philosophy will involve creating inclusive frameworks that respect cultural diversity while promoting universal human rights and ethical standards.

Advances in neuroscience are shedding new light on the nature of consciousness, challenging long-held philosophical assumptions. As scientists unravel the workings of the brain, philosophers will need to integrate these findings into theories of mind and consciousness.

Questions about free will, personal identity, and the nature of subjective experience will be re-examined in light of neuroscientific discoveries. The interdisciplinary dialogue between philosophy and neuroscience will be crucial in advancing our understanding of the human mind.

In the future, philosophy will increasingly engage with the public, addressing real-world issues and contributing to societal debates. Public philosophy, which seeks to make philosophical ideas accessible and relevant to a broader audience, will play a vital role in fostering critical thinking and informed citizenship. Philosophers will need to communicate their ideas through various media, participate in public discourse, and collaborate with other disciplines. By bridging the gap between academia and society, philosophy can remain a vital force in addressing contemporary challenges.

- **AI Ethics Boards**: In the future, AI ethics boards composed of philosophers, ethicists, and technologists may become a standard component of companies developing artificial intelligence. These boards will help navigate the ethical complexities of AI deployment, ensuring that AI systems align with human values and rights.
- **Neurophilosophy Institutes**: Dedicated institutes focusing on neurophilosophy may emerge, fostering collaboration between philosophers and neuroscientists. These institutes will explore the implications of brain research on concepts of consciousness, free will, and moral responsibility, potentially revolutionizing our understanding of the mind.
- **Global Philosophy Networks**: Advances in communication technology could lead to the creation of global philosophy networks, where scholars from different cultural and philosophical traditions collaborate on shared problems. These networks will promote cross-cultural dialogue and the development of more inclusive philosophical frameworks.
- **Environmental Ethics Certification**: As environmental concerns grow, there may be a rise in certification programs for businesses and policymakers in environmental ethics.

Philosophers will play a key role in developing and teaching these programs, ensuring that ethical considerations are integral to environmental decision-making.
- **Philosophical AI**: The development of advanced AI systems capable of engaging in philosophical reasoning and debate could become a reality. These AI philosophers could assist in exploring complex ethical dilemmas, offering diverse perspectives and potentially uncovering new insights into age-old philosophical questions.

The future of philosophy is poised to be dynamic and interdisciplinary, addressing the pressing issues of our time while continuing to explore the fundamental questions of human existence. As technology, society, and scientific knowledge evolve, philosophy will adapt and expand, remaining an essential field of inquiry and guidance in navigating the complexities of the modern world.

Did you know

That artificial intelligence is being used to create art and music, challenging traditional notions of creativity and authorship? AI algorithms can analyze vast amounts of data, learn artistic styles, and generate original compositions or visual artworks. This raises philosophical questions about the nature of creativity, the role of human intentionality in art, and the ethical implications of AI-generated works being sold and exhibited alongside human creations. As AI continues to develop, these debates will shape our understanding of what it means to be creative and the relationship between technology and artistic expression.

46. 20 Thought-provoking philosophy questions

1. **What is the nature of reality?**
   - Is reality objective and external, or is it subjective and constructed by our perceptions?

2. **Do humans have free will, or are our actions determined by external factors?**
   - Can we truly choose our actions, or are they predetermined by genetics, environment, and other influences?

3. **What is the meaning of life?**
   - Is there a universal purpose to human existence, or is meaning something we create individually?

4. **Is morality objective or subjective?**
   - Are there universal moral truths, or do morals vary based on culture, society, and personal perspective?

5. **What constitutes a just society?**
   - What principles should guide the organization of society to ensure fairness and justice for all?

6. **Can happiness be achieved through material wealth?**
   - Does the pursuit of material goods lead to true happiness, or are there more fulfilling paths to contentment?

7. **Is it possible to truly know anything for certain?**
   - How do we define knowledge, and can we ever attain absolute certainty about anything?

8. What is the nature of consciousness?

- What does it mean to be conscious, and how does consciousness arise from physical processes in the brain?

9. Do animals have rights?

- Should animals be afforded the same ethical considerations as humans, and if so, to what extent?

10. Is there life after death?

- What happens to us when we die, and can any form of existence continue after physical death?

11. What is the role of government in society?

- How much control should governments have over individuals, and what are the limits of state power?

12. Is beauty truly in the eye of the beholder?

- Are aesthetic judgments purely subjective, or are there objective standards of beauty?

13. Can war ever be justified?

- Under what circumstances, if any, is war morally permissible?

14. What is the nature of time?

- Is time a fundamental aspect of the universe, or is it a construct of human perception?

15. Do we have a duty to future generations?

- What ethical obligations do we have to ensure the well-being of future people?

16. What is the relationship between mind and body?

- How do our mental states relate to our physical states, and can one exist without the other?

17. Is it better to be just or to appear just?

- Should one strive for genuine virtue, or is it sufficient to merely appear virtuous in society?

18. What is the nature of happiness?

- How do we define happiness, and what are the most effective ways to achieve it?

19. What is the significance of art in human life?

- Why do humans create and value art, and what role does it play in our understanding of the world?

20. Are we obligated to help others in need?

- What are our moral responsibilities toward others, particularly those who are less fortunate?

These questions cover a wide range of philosophical topics, encouraging deep reflection and stimulating rich discussions on fundamental aspects of human existence and society.

47. The Mandela Effect

The Mandela Effect is a fascinating psychological phenomenon where a large group of people collectively remember something differently from how it occurred. The term was coined by Fiona Broome in 2009 after she discovered that many people, including herself, incorrectly remembered Nelson Mandela dying in prison during the 1980s, when in fact he was released and went on to become the President of South Africa. This collective false memory sparked discussions and investigations into why such widespread inaccuracies in memory occur.

One of the intriguing aspects of the Mandela Effect is how it reveals the fallibility and malleability of human memory. Often, these false memories are so vivid and detailed that people are convinced they are accurate. This phenomenon has led to various theories about the nature of reality and memory, including the idea of parallel universes or alternate realities. While these theories are speculative and not widely accepted in the scientific community, they capture the imagination and underscore the mysterious nature of memory.

The Mandela Effect extends beyond just the memory of Nelson Mandela. It encompasses a wide range of instances where large groups of people remember events, details, or facts incorrectly. These can range from lines in famous movies to brand logos and historical events. The common thread is that these false memories are shared by a significant number of people, making them more than just individual errors in recall.

Examples of the Mandela Effect

1. **Nelson Mandela's Death**: Many remember him dying in prison during the 1980s.
2. **Berenstain Bears**: Recalled as "Berenstein Bears" by many.

3. **Looney Tunes**: Often remembered as "Looney Toons."
4. **Curious George**: Some believe he had a tail.
5. **Febreze**: Recalled as "Febreeze."
6. **Oscar Mayer**: Remembered as "Oscar Meyer."
7. **Mona Lisa's Smile**: Thought to be different than it is.
8. **C-3PO's Leg**: Some remember him having two gold legs, but one is silver.
9. **Pikachu's Tail**: Believed to have a black tip at the end.
10. **KitKat**: Remembered with a hyphen (Kit-Kat).
11. **Fruit of the Loom**: Thought to have a cornucopia in the logo.
12. **"Luke, I am your father"**: Misquoted as "No, I am your father."
13. **Mr. Monopoly's Monocle**: Remembered as having one, but he does not.
14. **"We Are the Champions"**: Many recall the song ending with "of the world," which it doesn't.
15. **The Flintstones**: Often misspelled as "The Flinstones."
16. **Chartreuse**: Some believe it to be a shade of red or pink, but it's green.
17. **"Hello, Clarice"**: Misremembered line from "The Silence of the Lambs."
18. **Life is like a box of chocolates**: Correct line is "Life was like a box of chocolates."
19. **Smokey Bear**: Often misremembered as "Smokey the Bear."
20. **Queen's "We Will Rock You"**: Some recall the song ending differently.

The Science Behind the Mandela Effect

The Mandela Effect can be explained through several psychological mechanisms and theories. One prominent explanation is the concept of **false memories**, which occur when the brain tries to fill in gaps in our memory with plausible information. This can be influenced by suggestive questioning, social interactions, or simply the passage of time. Our memories are not perfect recordings; they are reconstructed each time we recall them, making them susceptible to alteration.

Another contributing factor is **confabulation**, where the brain creates fabricated memories without the intention to deceive. This can happen when we integrate pieces of various memories into a coherent, though inaccurate, whole. **Source monitoring errors** also play a role; this is when we confuse the source of a memory, attributing it to the wrong context or time.

The **social and cultural factors** can also amplify the Mandela Effect. When a large group of people shares the same incorrect memory, it can reinforce and validate the false recollection. This collective reinforcement can make the incorrect memory feel more authentic and widespread, further entrenching it in the public consciousness.

In essence, the Mandela Effect highlights the complex and often unreliable nature of human memory. It serves as a reminder that our recollections are not infallible and are influenced by various psychological and social factors. Understanding these mechanisms can help us appreciate the limitations of memory and the importance of corroborating our recollections with factual evidence.

48. The Concept of Free Will

The concept of free will has been a central topic in philosophy for centuries, raising profound questions about human autonomy, moral responsibility, and the nature of the universe. Philosophers have debated whether our actions are determined by causal laws or if we have the ability to choose freely, independent of external influences. This debate encompasses various perspectives, from determinism and compatibilism to libertarianism.

Determinism

Determinism posits that every event or state of affairs, including human actions, is determined by preceding events in accordance with universal laws. Under this view, free will is an illusion, as everything that happens is the result of a causal chain.

Baron d'Holbach: In his work "The System of Nature" (1770), d'Holbach argued that humans are completely determined by their environment, biology, and upbringing. He famously stated, "Man's life is a line that nature commands him to describe upon the surface of the earth, without ever being able to swerve from it, even for an instant."

Spinoza: Baruch Spinoza, in his "Ethics," also adopted a deterministic view, asserting that free will is an illusion. He wrote, "Men think themselves free, because they are conscious of their actions and ignorant of the causes by which they are determined."

Libertarianism

Libertarianism, in contrast, argues that humans possess free will and that our choices are not determined by prior states of the world. According to this view, individuals have the capacity to act otherwise in a given situation.

Jean-Paul Sartre: Jean-Paul Sartre, a prominent existentialist philosopher, believed in absolute free will. In his seminal work "Being and Nothingness," he wrote, "Man is condemned to be free; because once thrown into the world, he is responsible for everything he does." Sartre emphasized that with freedom comes the burden of responsibility, and individuals must create their own essence through actions.

Roderick Chisholm: Chisholm, a 20th-century philosopher, argued for agent causation, where individuals are the true originators of their actions. He said, "Each of us, when we act, is a prime mover unmoved. We are, in our actions, not merely a part of the causal chain, but the originators of new causal chains."

Compatibilism

Compatibilism seeks to reconcile free will and determinism, asserting that free will is compatible with a deterministic universe. Compatibilists argue that free will exists if individuals can act according to their desires and intentions, even if these are causally determined.

David Hume: David Hume, an early proponent of compatibilism, argued in "An Enquiry Concerning Human Understanding" that free will is compatible with determinism. He stated, "By liberty, then, we can only mean a power of acting or not acting, according to the determinations of the will; that is, if we choose to remain at rest, we may; if we choose to move, we also may."

John Locke: John Locke contributed to the compatibilist view by suggesting that freedom is the ability to act according to one's own will. In his "Essay Concerning Human Understanding," he wrote, "The liberty of man, in society, is to be under no other legislative power but that established by consent in the commonwealth; nor under the dominion of any will, or restraint of any law, but what that legislative shall enact according to the trust put in it.

Modern philosophers continue to explore the concept of free will, often incorporating findings from neuroscience and psychology. The debate remains vibrant, with ongoing discussions about the implications of free will for moral responsibility and the justice system.

Daniel Dennett: Dennett, a contemporary philosopher, defends a compatibilist view in his book "Freedom Evolves." He argues that free will is not about absolute independence from causality but about the ability to act in accordance with one's character and reasoning. He writes, "The varieties of free will worth wanting are all compatible with determinism."

Sam Harris: Sam Harris, a neuroscientist and philosopher, argues against the existence of free will in his book "Free Will." He asserts that our thoughts and intentions are products of unconscious causes, and thus, true free will is an illusion. Harris states, "Free will is an illusion so convincing that people simply refuse to believe that we don't have it."

1. **Neuroscientific Studies**: Some neuroscientific studies, such as those by Benjamin Libet, suggest that brain activity predicting a decision occurs before the individual becomes consciously aware of making the decision. This has raised questions about the nature of free will and the role of consciousness in decision-making.
2. **Legal Implications**: The debate over free will has significant implications for the legal system. If determinism is true, it challenges traditional notions of moral responsibility and punishment. Some legal scholars argue for a re-evaluation of how culpability and responsibility are assigned.
3. **Cultural Variations**: Different cultures have varying beliefs about free will. Western cultures often emphasize individual autonomy, while some Eastern philosophies, like Buddhism, focus on interconnectedness and the idea that free will is limited by karma and the conditions of existence.
4. **Quantum Mechanics**: Some proponents of free will argue that quantum mechanics, with its inherent indeterminacy, allows for the possibility of free will. However, this remains a contentious point, as randomness does not necessarily equate to control or freedom.

59. The Hawthorne Effect

The Hawthorne Effect is a psychological phenomenon where individuals alter their behavior due to their awareness of being observed. This effect was first identified during a series of studies conducted at the Hawthorne Works, a Western Electric factory in Cicero, Illinois, in the 1920s and 1930s. The researchers discovered that workers' productivity increased when they were observed, regardless of the changes made to their working conditions. The Hawthorne Effect highlights the impact that the presence of observers or perceived attention can have on individuals' performance and behavior.

Study Overview: The Hawthorne Studies

The Hawthorne Studies were a series of experiments conducted from 1924 to 1932 at the Western Electric Hawthorne Works. These studies aimed to understand how different working conditions affected worker productivity. The most notable parts of these studies were the illumination experiments, the relay assembly test room studies, and the bank wiring observation room studies.

Illumination Experiments

The initial studies were designed to examine the impact of lighting on worker productivity. Researchers altered the levels of illumination in the work environment to see how it affected output. Surprisingly, productivity improved under both increased and decreased lighting conditions. This unexpected result led researchers to suspect that the real factor influencing productivity was the attention given to the workers, not the lighting itself. The mere act of being observed and the special attention workers received during the experiments seemed to boost their productivity.

Relay Assembly Test Room Studies

In another phase of the study, researchers isolated a small group of female workers who assembled telephone relays. Various changes were made to their work conditions, including different work hours, break times, and incentives. Regardless of the specific changes, productivity generally increased. This suggested that the workers' performance was more influenced by the social and psychological factors of being observed and receiving attention from the researchers rather than by the physical changes to their working conditions.

Bank Wiring Observation Room Studies

The bank wiring observation room studies focused on a group of male workers in the bank wiring room. Unlike the previous studies, this one found that productivity did not increase in the same way. This suggested that the Hawthorne Effect may vary depending on the context and the individuals involved. The social dynamics and informal group norms among the workers played a significant role in their behavior. The workers developed their own norms and standards for productivity, which were influenced by peer interactions more than by the researchers' presence.

Findings

The Hawthorne Studies concluded that social factors, attention from researchers, and the feeling of being valued played a crucial role in worker productivity. The studies emphasized the importance of considering human relations and psychological factors in the workplace, leading to the development of the Human Relations Movement in management theory. This movement highlighted the need for managers to focus on social and emotional aspects of work life, not just the physical working conditions.

5 Crazy Facts About the Hawthorne Effect

1. Origin in Illumination Studies:
- The initial studies were designed to examine the impact of lighting on worker productivity. Surprisingly, productivity improved under both increased and decreased lighting, leading researchers to suspect that the attention given to workers was the real factor.

2. Observer Impact:
- The Hawthorne Effect suggests that simply being observed can make people work harder and perform better, even if no other changes are made to their environment or tasks.

3. Wider Implications:
- Beyond the workplace, the Hawthorne Effect is observed in various fields such as education, healthcare, and social research, influencing the way studies and interventions are designed and interpreted.

4. Short-Lived Impact:
- The boost in productivity due to the Hawthorne Effect is often temporary. Once the novelty of being observed wears off, individuals may revert to their usual behavior.

5. Influence on Modern Research:
- The Hawthorne Effect has led to the development of more rigorous experimental designs, such as double-blind studies,

to minimize the influence of observation on participants' behavior.

Despite the significant insights provided by the Hawthorne Studies, there are several limitations to consider. One major limitation is the ambiguity in the interpretation of results. The studies involved multiple changes in working conditions, such as variations in lighting, work hours, and breaks, making it challenging to isolate the specific factors that influenced productivity. This multifaceted approach has led to debates over whether the observed productivity gains were truly due to the Hawthorne Effect or other variables.

Another limitation is the lack of rigorous control in the experimental design. The studies did not employ the strict methodological controls that are standard in modern psychological research. For instance, there was no control group that was not subjected to any changes or observation, which makes it difficult to rule out other potential causes for the observed changes in behavior. This has led some researchers to question the validity and reliability of the findings.

The small sample sizes and specific demographic groups used in the studies also limit the generalizability of the results. Most of the experiments focused on small groups of workers within a single factory, and many involved only female workers in specific roles. This narrow focus raises questions about whether the findings can be applied broadly across different industries, job roles, or diverse populations.

Furthermore, the studies were conducted in a particular historical and cultural context. The social and economic environment of the 1920s and 1930s was markedly different from today's workplace conditions. The extent to which the Hawthorne Effect can be observed in contemporary settings with advanced technology, different work cultures, and modern management practices remains a topic of ongoing research and debate.

Finally, the temporary nature of the productivity boost observed in the studies highlights another limitation. The increased productivity often waned once the novelty of being observed wore off. This suggests that while the Hawthorne Effect can lead to short-term improvements, it may not result in sustained long-term changes in behavior or performance. This ephemeral impact underscores the need for continuous engagement and attention to maintain productivity gains.

Overall, while the Hawthorne Studies have been foundational in highlighting the importance of social and psychological factors in the workplace, their limitations suggest that further research with more rigorous methodologies is necessary to fully understand the complexities of the Hawthorne Effect and its implications for modern organizational practices.

"The Hawthorne Effect continues to remind us that how we observe and interact with individuals can profoundly impact their behavior, a lesson applicable across various fields from psychology to organizational management."

Thank You Note

Thank you for choosing **"Intelligent Minds: Psychology & Philosophy Trivia Book."** We hope that your journey through the intricate landscapes of psychology and philosophy has been as enriching and thought-provoking as we intended. Your curiosity and willingness to explore these profound subjects keep the spirit of inquiry alive.

We extend our deepest gratitude to the philosophers, psychologists, and thinkers whose work inspired this book. Their contributions continue to shape our understanding of the human mind and the complexities of existence.

To our readers, your engagement and reflections on these topics are invaluable. Whether you are a student, a lifelong learner, or someone passionate about these fields, your interest and participation in these discussions help advance the collective knowledge and understanding of our society.

We hope that this book has not only provided you with knowledge but also sparked new questions and insights. Remember, the journey of learning and discovery never truly ends. Continue to question, explore, and seek out new perspectives.

Thank you for being a part of this intellectual adventure. We look forward to accompanying you on many more journeys through the fascinating worlds of psychology and philosophy.

Scan the QR code to access exclusive free content and resources.

If you enjoyed this book, **please leave a review on Amazon** and share your thoughts. Your feedback helps us continue to provide engaging and insightful content.

Printed in Great Britain
by Amazon